CW01418402

# Little Laureates

# **Poems From South Yorkshire**
## Edited by Allison Jones

**Young Writers**

First published in Great Britain in 2008 by:
Young Writers
Remus House
Coltsfoot Drive
Peterborough
PE2 9JX
Telephone: 01733 890066
Website: www.youngwriters.co.uk

SB ISBN 978-1 84431 480 5

# Foreword

Young Writers was established in 1991 and has been passionately devoted to the promotion of reading and writing in children and young adults ever since. The quest continues today. Young Writers remains as committed to the nurturing of poetic and literary talent as ever.

This year's Young Writers competition has proven as vibrant and dynamic as ever and we are delighted to present a showcase of the best poetry from across the UK and in some cases overseas. Each poem has been selected from a wealth of *Little Laureates* entries before ultimately being published in this, our sixteenth primary school poetry series.

Once again, we have been supremely impressed by the overall quality of the entries we have received. The imagination, energy and creativity which has gone into each young writer's entry made choosing the poems a challenging and often difficult but ultimately hugely rewarding task - the general high standard of the work submitted ensured this opportunity to bring their poetry to a larger appreciative audience.

We sincerely hope you are pleased with this final collection and that you will enjoy *Little Laureates Poems From South Yorkshire* for many years to come.

# Contents

## Holy Cross Deanery Primary School

| | |
|---|---|
| Sheldon Leigh Hirst  (10) | 31 |
| Lisa Wilcock  (10) | 32 |
| Lewis Kelk  (10) | 32 |
| Chloe Bent  (9) | 32 |
| Liam Woodcock  (10) | 32 |
| Ellis Higgins  (10) | 33 |
| Ciara Owen  (11) | 33 |
| Brandon Semmens  (11) | 33 |
| Curtis Firth  (10) | 33 |
| Brent Barraclough  (10) | 34 |
| Ellie Clarkson  (10) | 34 |
| Brittany Callaghan  (9) | 34 |
| Rebekah Morley  (9) | 35 |
| Chloe Harpin  (10) | 35 |
| Liam Lindley  (11) | 35 |
| Reece Hamer  (10) | 35 |

## Limpsfield Junior School

| | |
|---|---|
| Daniel Thorpe  (9) | 36 |
| Charlotte Slack  (10) | 36 |
| Liam Ashton  (7) | 37 |
| Sophie Hurt  (10) | 37 |
| Emily-Rose Bower  (9) | 38 |
| Lucas Cawthorne | 38 |
| Josh Parker  (10) | 39 |
| Jack Kazmierkiewicz  (9) | 39 |
| Megan Oliver  (9) | 40 |
| Shaiyan Moss  (11) | 41 |
| Daniel Whiteman  (7) | 42 |
| Cameron Hizam  (8) | 42 |
| James Bonnett  (10) | 43 |
| Dannielle Snee  (8) | 44 |
| Stacey Mazorodze  (7) | 45 |
| Chloe Needham  (7) | 46 |
| Hollie Bower  (8) | 47 |
| Caitlin Moore  (7) | 48 |
| Jomana Mare  (7) | 48 |
| Nicole Lindsay  (8) | 49 |
| Jessica Beck  (7) | 49 |

Bryn Wainwright  (7)                               50
Liam Claricoats  (7)                               51


**Montagu Junior School**
Bethany McCall  (8)                                51
Joshua Troop  (9)                                  52
Danielle Poole  (8)                                52
Darren Pearson  (9)                                53
Callum Bater  (8)                                  53
Emily Hargreaves  (8)                              54
Shelby Gilliver  (8)                               54
Cara Bennett  (8)                                  55
George Goodinson  (8)                              55
Shannon Ferguson-Corrie  (10)                      56
Louis Finney  (9)                                  57
Laura Gibbons  (8)                                 58


**St Joseph's Catholic Primary School, Doncaster**
Louis Moore  (10)                                  58
Sofia Calzini  (8)                                 59
Holly Wilson  (8)                                  59
Stephanie Gillespie  (10)                          60
Laurence Anthony  (8)                              60
Mark Donnelly  (10)                                61
Callum Godley  (8)                                 61
Hannah Duffy  (11)                                 62
Amy Lynch  (9)                                     62
Alex Charlesworth  (11)                            63
Declan McMenamin  (8)                              63
Liam Gormley  (8)                                  64
Jasmine West  (8)                                  64
Lauren Forest  (11)                                65
Alex Godley  (8)                                   65
Jordan Saunders  (8)                               65
Heather Lukins  (10)                               66
Haydn Ellis  (10)                                  66
Jonjo Hall  (8)                                    67
Katie Harvey  (10)                                 67
Emerald Young  (10)                                67
Enya Samways  (10)                                 68
Caitlin Isle  (10)                                 68

Joe Dockerty  (10)                          69
Zoe Neocleous  (10)                         69
Hannelore Southern  (10)                    70
Natalie McMenamin  (10)                     70
Aimee Vickers  (8)                          70
Emilio Marcos Sierra  (10)                  71
Edward Allen  (11)                          71
Joseph Stannard  (10)                       71
Georgia Harper  (11)                        72
Georgia Wren  (10)                          72
Bronagh Gunn  (11)                          73
Luke Scollins  (10)                         73
Daniel Johnson  (11)                        74
Paige Simpson  (8)                          74
Grace Fielding  (8)                         75
Hannah Russell  (11)                        75

## St Marie's Catholic Primary School, Sheffield

Elizabeth Martin  (8)                       76
Francesca Thomas  (8)                       77
Isaac McQuinn  (8)                          77
Daisy Shemmelds  (8)                        77
Rebecca Shiel  (8)                          78
Niamh Farrell  (8)                          78
Georgia Oldfield  (8)                       78
Hugh Hackney  (8)                           79
JD Quinn                                    79
Alice Reddin  (8)                           79
Ian Mercado  (10)                           80
Elizabeth Briddock  (8)                     80
Morgan Simpson  (8)                         80
Cameron Colclough  (8)                      81
Guido Teruzzi  (8)                          81
Rosey Rostant  (8)                          81
Dominic Casey  (11)                         82
Theresa Staub  (9)                          82
Bethany Kirkbride  (10)                     83
Katherine Rice  (10)                        83
Jack Clohessy  (10)                         83
Ifeoma Ezepue  (10)                         84
Katie Farrell  (11)                         85

Niamh Grant  (8)                                                    85
Agatha Milner  (10)                                                 86
Martha Scattergood & Eleri Kirkpatrick-Lorente  (9)                87
Ryan Tweddell  (8)                                                  87

## St Theresa's Catholic Primary School, Sheffield

Reece Major  (8)                                                   87
Hannah O'Rourke & Alicia Farrell  (10)                            88
Megan Torpey  (8)                                                 88
Kieran Beer  (9)                                                  88
Chloe Timms  (11)                                                89
Courtney Wright  (8)                                             89
Ellie-Marie Ottewell  (8)                                       89
Annie Wood  (10)                                                90
Hana Riaz  (9)                                                   90
John Zurita  (11)                                                91
Tyler Brown  (8)                                                 91
Tumi Gopalang  (10)                                             92
Jordan Barnes  (10)                                             92
Kaine Wild  (10)                                                93
Joe McNally  (10)                                                93
Kiera Burgin  (11)                                              94
Hannah Miles  (10)                                              94
Erica Bothamley  (10)                                          95
Imogen Norcliffe  (8)                                           95
Jordan Scarborough  (11)                                       96
Harry Atkinson  (10)                                            96
Hannah O'Rourke  (10)                                          97
Mollie Wood  (10)                                               97
Jordan Loftus  (11)                                             98
Sharna Burgin  (8)                                              98
Danielle Platton  (10)                                          99
Ashley Lane  (8)                                                99
Libia Mae Stachiw  (8)                                         100
Charlotte Colk  (9)                                            100
Nathan Mason  (9)                                              100
Shelby-Jo Chambers  (8)                                       101

## Shafton Primary School

Corie Wagstaffe  (10)                                         101
Chloe Lindley  (7)                                            101

Holly Lockwood  (10)                  102
Bethany Cawston  (9)                  102
Connor Cocks  (8)                     103
Daniel Sykes  (7)                     103
Alex Goddard  (11)                    104
Jake Arrowsmith  (8)                  104
Lewisham Screaton  (10)               104
Elizabeth Wignall  (10)               105
Ryan Hewitt  (11)                     105
Kyle Cooper  (10)                     105
Becky Hirst  (10)                     106
Alice Whittaker  (10)                 106
Jack Sephton  (8)                     107
Thomas Birkin  (10)                   107
Harry Francis  (7)                    108
Lewis Briggs  (10)                    108
Megan Hamer  (11)                     109
Myles Goddard  (8)                    109
Jacob Millard  (10)                   109
Kristie Shelton  (10)                 110
Georgie-Lee Chapman  (9)             110
Lewis Horsbrough  (8)                 110
Sasha Haynes  (8)                     111
Jordan Hinchliffe  (8)                111
Kieren Saxton  (8)                    111

## Waverley Primary School

Kenny Sweeney  (7)                    112
Eyea Ballah  (7)                      112
Ian Rathbone  (7)                     112
Nicole Spencer  (8)                   113
Ashley Law  (7)                       113
Alex Jenkinson  (7)                   113
Shona Brown  (7)                      114
Olivia Hartle  (7)                    115
Chloe Hawcroft  (8)                   116
Tia Katey Gleadall  (7)              116
Nathan Morgan  (8)                    116
Rayanne Basley-Cox  (7)              117
Natasha Morgan  (8)                   117

## Willow Primary School

| | |
|---|---|
| Javian Abiad  (9) | 117 |
| Laura McKirdy  (9) | 118 |
| William Feborov  (8) | 118 |
| Lakhpreet Kaur  (8) | 119 |
| Liana Haynes  (8) | 119 |
| Sidney Choi  (9) | 120 |
| Phoebe Ramsbottom  (8) | 120 |
| Shane Salmon  (9) | 121 |
| Hannah Skipp  (9) | 122 |
| Paige Durdy  (9) | 122 |
| Elliott Tong  (9) | 123 |
| Lauren Playfoot  (8) | 123 |
| Maxwell Abbott  (8) | 123 |
| Adam Wilson & Danial Mohammed  (10) | 124 |
| Millie Gilkes  (9) | 124 |
| Josh Horgan & James Sneddon  (10) | 125 |
| Sophie Marsh  (8) | 125 |
| Class 6W (Age 10 & 11) | 126 |
| Max Green  (9) | 126 |
| Simon Stockwell & Ralf Hudson  (10) | 127 |
| Imogen Moore & Daniel Hassell  (10) | 127 |
| Katie McGlone  (10) | 128 |
| Lewis Bennett  (9) | 128 |
| Ryan Lambert & Ryan Geldard  (10) | 129 |
| Courtney Chalk  (9) | 129 |
| Jordenne Murray  (10) | 130 |
| Grace Wood  (9) | 130 |
| Robyn Gunn  (9) | 131 |
| Georgia Lakin & Duncan Haddrell  (10) | 132 |
| Chloe Cope & Sophia Arjomand  (11) | 132 |
| Jenny Collins  (11) & James Peach  (10) | 133 |
| Danny Young  (10) & Becky Smith | 133 |
| Joshua Bennett  (10) & Emma Phagra | 134 |
| Olivia Binns & Afnan Rabbani  (10) | 134 |
| Lewis Mycock & Ellie Neil  (11) | 135 |

# The Poems

# I Want To Paint

I want to paint a shimmering sunbeam
Sitting silently.

I want to paint a dancing teddy
Talking like a car engine.

I want to paint a jigging doll,
Jigging.

I want to paint a lazy Donald Duck
Dancing delicately.

I want to paint a golden glimmering fairy,
Sprinkling magic dust.

I want to paint a smiling snow white dancing display.

I want to paint a cute cat creeping courageously.

**Courtney Wheeler  (8)**
**Beck Primary School**


# I Want To Paint

I want to paint a banana moon
Shimmering in the freezing cold light.

I want to paint a magical fairy
With a sparkling dress.

I want to paint a bird
With golden paint.

I want to paint an American cowboy and horse.

I want to paint an egg partying with a spoon.

I want to paint a guinea pig
Singing with fish.

I want to paint an Italian Pizza man in Italy.

I want to paint a vicious bear.

**Megan Reed  (9)**
**Beck Primary School**

# I Saw

I saw a golden eagle
Shining in the sun.

I saw a golden turtle
As fast as a rocket.

I saw a golden monkey
Swimming the English Channel.

I saw a golden tree
Digging its way through Earth.

I saw a cheeky cheetah
Cheating at chess.

I saw a magical monkey
Messing with me.

**Thomas Frith  (8)**
**Beck Primary School**


# I Want To Paint

I want to paint a silver bird
Dancing in the sun.

I want to paint swirling seashells
Slipping slowly.

I want to paint a glittery lava lamp
To lighten my thoughts.

I want to paint singing and dancing fairies.

I want to paint a cowboy
Sunbathing on the beach.

I want to paint white snow
Falling from the sky.

**Summer Farnell  (8)**
**Beck Primary School**

# What Is The Moon?

The moon is a crystal ball
On a fluffy black pillow.

It is a white bottle top
Shining in the dark.

The moon is a giant torch
Shining in a dark cave.

It is a white football
In the night-time sky.

The moon is a bowl of cheese
In a very dark kitchen.

It is a white banana
In a dark fruit bowl.

**Courtney Rogan  (9)**
**Beck Primary School**


# Richard Fryer

Richard Fryer
Richard Fryer
Stuck his leg in a tumble dryer.

Tumble dryer
Tumble dryer
Left and right went Richard Fryer.

Richard Fryer
Richard Fryer
A boy with his leg in a tumble dryer.

Tumble dryer
Tumble dryer
Last home of Richard Fryer.

**Callum Norrie  (7)**
**Beck Primary School**

# The Garden

Pretty flowers dancing like the Queen.
Brown wooden bench sunbathing silently.
Green trees growing in the grass.
Long worms relaxing in the mud.
Small tomatoes growing naturally.
Soft green leaves growing in nature.
Autumn leaves crunching underfoot
Big brown trees
Laughing funny flowers.
Butterflies' wings beating like drums.
Brown benches talking to the future.

**Chelsea Riley  (8)**
**Beck Primary School**


# The Lion

The lion is a huge ball of fire
Rolling through the golden-brown savannah.

He has powerful daggers
Shredding his prey to pieces.

He has amber jewels
Sparkling like a golden medal.

He has silver blood-covered needles.

**Charley Booth & Brandon Jones  (9)**
**Beck Primary School**


# I Saw

I saw a fast motorbike drive a man.
I saw a dog walking a man.
I saw a whale wearing people's clothes.
I saw a silly-looking alien talking to the whole school.

**Reagan Wildon  (8)**
**Beck Primary School**

## Secret Wishes

I wish I would never grow up
And that I could capture my childhood
And keep it forever.

I wish my hair was as white as snow
So it would be winter for my hair.

I wish I could capture the sound of bubble wrap
Popping like sizzling popcorn.

**Lorna Hadley (8)**
**Beck Primary School**


## Secret Wishes

I wish I could have a chocolate world
As if I lived in a chocolate bar
And I could eat all of my house if I got hungry.

I wish I could have a soft bed
Like a pillow to keep my thoughts locked up safe.

I wish I could have a world with no rules
So I could run riot like a dog with no lead.

**Summer Hawnt (9)**
**Beck Primary School**


## Secret Wishes

I wish I could capture a glittering rainbow
And hide it in my PE bag.

I wish I could touch an Arabian pony
Who was as swift as the wind.

I wish I could see
A magic carpet that would whisk me away to dreamland.

**Isabel Edain (8)**
**Beck Primary School**

## Secret Wishes

I wish I could capture my dog's bark
So I could listen to it when I wanted to.

I wish I could capture a chocolate fountain
So I could keep it to myself.

I wish I could capture millions of rolling pizzas
Falling from the sky,
So I could eat them all.

I wish I could capture helium balloons
So I could fly up into space with nobody else.

I wish I could capture a million pounds from the sky,
So I could spend it on myself.

**Hannah Yeardley  (8)**
**Beck Primary School**


## I Saw

I saw a man flying a white angel.

I saw a daft dolphin dipping in the dictionary.

I saw a purple puppy playing with her posh pumpkin.

I saw a handsome shark
Dancing in a pub.

I saw a bursting volcano exploring
Like a dog very angry.

I saw a cheating cheetah
Cheating at chess.

I saw the sun shouting at the clouds.

**Leah Fish  (8)**
**Beck Primary School**

# I Saw

I saw the moon look like a pie.
I saw a volcano shoot hot bubbling chocolate.
I saw a shark riding a volcanic skateboard.
I saw a monkey riding a bike without stopping.

I saw a spotty giraffe kissing a horse.
I saw a hairy hippo belly-bounce on water.
I saw a house as big as a turnip.
I saw the wind blow over a rhinoceros
Like a mad tornado.

I saw a hairy bull trying to get a pack
Of cheese and onion crisps.
I saw a cheetah cheat at chess.
I saw a tiger tidying.

**Jacob Etherton  (9)**
Beck Primary School


# I Saw

I saw a posh puppy playing ping pong.

I saw a great white shark dancing
In a nightclub like a pop star.

I saw a house talking all day long
To the sun

I saw a baby lion cub glancing all day long
At the sunny sun.

I saw an ant scaring a dinosaur
But the dinosaur said, 'Don't scare me!'

I saw a rumbling rhinoceros rioting
In a rugby match.

**Kiyani Clayton  (8)**
Beck Primary School

# Secret Wishes

I wish I could capture a beautiful chocolate fountain
So I could have strawberries and runny chocolate after tea.

I wish I could capture birds' voices
So it would make me go to sleep.

I wish I could capture lots of money falling from a hotel
So I could get lots of clothes and shoes.

I wish I could capture a bee
So it would make me some honey in a jar.

I wish I could capture butterflies' wings
So I could put them in a plastic bottle.

**Olivia Page-Turner  (8)**
**Beck Primary School**


# I Saw

I saw an automatic blackbird
Dancing on a tiny piece of shell.

I saw a comfy marshmallow house
Walking very gently like a huge cushion.

I saw a clear white fluffy cloud
Floating like a balloon on its way to the far north.

I saw Miss McLuskie eating a silly-looking pizza
From out of space made from aliens.

I saw a colourful bowl of fruit bouncing up and down
Like a ball.

**Ramsha Ahmed  (9)**
**Beck Primary School**

# I Saw

I saw a human's body shaped like a dog's body.

I saw a hippo popping like madness.

I saw a flying kitten being bad.

I saw a kitten popping like crazy chickens.

I saw a giant pony singing to its puppy,
The puppy was cute.

I saw one hundred pens and diaries
Dropping like raindrops.

I saw my family getting back together again.

I saw my own dreams in the mirror.

**Bethan Prosser  (9)**
**Beck Primary School**


# Secret Wishes

I wish I could capture all of the best characters
From High School Musical
Because I want to learn their songs and dances.

I wish I could capture a chocolate brown fountain
And give most of it to the poor charity.

I wish I could capture five guinea pigs
And give one to my family in my house.

I wish I could capture lots of Hollywood pop stars
And let them draw their faces and autographs on my wall.

**Rebecca Woods  (8)**
**Beck Primary School**

## Secret Wishes

I wish I could capture a sparkling rainbow
So that I could paint pictures whenever I wanted.

I wish I could capture a swooping pony
Falling from the sky.

I wish I could capture the sound of sea rushing
So it could make me up in the morning.

I wish I could capture a wrestler
So he could teach me how to wrestle
So I could become the greatest wrestler ever,
And bring joy to the children.

**Ryan German  (8)**
**Beck Primary School**


## What Is The Moon

The moon is a mysterious ball of pleasant white
Hovering in the dark sky.

The moon is shimmering like a speeding bullet
Out of a really big black gun.

The moon is a ball going in a big black net.

**Charlie Whiteley  (9)**
**Beck Primary School**


## Secret Wishes

I wish I could have fireball powers
Like the stars.

I wish I could capture a twinkling star.

I wish I could capture a chocolate ruler
And a chocolate pencil.

**Ellis McGrath  (8)**
**Beck Primary School**

## Secret Wishes

I wish I could see a chocolate world
Like me living in a nutty crunchy chocolate bar.

I wish I could fly like a beautiful hummingbird
So I could go and see my friend straight after school.

I wish I could have a million pets in the universe
Like living on a farm.

I wish I could have golden time every day
Like living in a golden world.

**Hannah Walker  (8)**
Beck Primary School

## Secret Wishes

I wish I could capture the sound of bubble wrap
Popping like popcorn.

I wish I could see the sky as rich
As brown chocolate.

I wish I could feel a bed as
Soft as a thousand feathers.

I wish I could chew a chocolate pencil
Like a Galaxy bar.

**Hannah Bruney  (8)**
Beck Primary School

## Secret Wishes

I wish I could capture thunder and lightning
Like crunchy leaves in a bag.

I wish I could taste the end of my pencil
Like Galaxy chocolate.

I wish the entire world was made out of chocolate.

**Levi Cook  (9)**
Beck Primary School

# What Is The Moon?

The moon is a white dish,
On a clean black cloth.

It is a round crystal ball,
In a piece of coal.

The moon is white paint dripping,
In a cave that is pitch-black.

It is a giant torch in space,
Looking down on us.

The moon is a ball of cheese,
In a black fridge.

It is a snowman standing in the dark.

The moon is a cloud what has gone into a round ball
At night and it is dark.

**Ellen Lee  (9)**
**Beck Primary School**


# Secret Wishes

I wish I could see
No nasty people in the world.

I wish I could capture the words
Of my turtle talking like flowers rubbing
Against my face.

I wish I could hold a star
Like a burning sunbeam.

I wish the water bottles were filled
With melted chocolate
No more dinner times.

**Amber Macpherson  (8)**
**Beck Primary School**

# Secret Wishes

I wish
I could capture a bike.

I wish
I could capture a chocolate ball.

I wish
I was as big as a man.

I wish
I could fly like a bird.

I wish
I was Lego.

I wish
There was no men or women
Who were bad.

I wish
I could have every bit of money.

I wish
I was the boss of the world.

I wish
I was a little boss.

**Thomas Vaughan  (8)**
**Beck Primary School**


# Secret Wishes

I wish I could fly like a booster rocket
Up to Mars.

I wish I could capture tiny people
Like ants and watch them.

I wish I could dive
Into a chocolate sea.

**Laud Moore  (8)**
**Beck Primary School**

# Secret Wishes

I wish I could capture a rainbow
And keep it in my bag.

I wish I could capture some chocolate pencils
And nibble at them when I am working.

I wish I could capture a sizzling sunbeam
Like popcorn popping in a pan.

I wish I could capture everything
And the world was made of chocolate.

**Dominic Younis  (8)**
**Beck Primary School**


# Secret Wishes

I wish I could hear motors like cars revving.

I wish I could see an enormous swimming pool
Like a wave splashing.

I wish I could capture a hundred thousand
And keep it under my pillow.

I wish I could be a footballer
And play for Man United.

**Jack Hattersley  (8)**
**Beck Primary School**


# Secret Wishes

I wish I could capture a piece of the cloud
And keep it like birds tweeting.

I wish I had a driver's licence
So I could drive a car.

**Riley Wigley  (8)**
**Beck Primary School**

# Secret Wishes

I wish I could be a yellow roller coaster
That goes up and down the loops.

I wish I could be on a big wheel
That would turn around and round.

I wish I could be the water shoot.

I wish I could be a runaway train
Which would take me to Ingoldmells.

**Andrew Saxon  (8)**
Beck Primary School


# Secret Wishes

I wish I could touch a bright twinkling star
And it would look like my diamond earring.

I wish I could pop bubble wrap
And make a little bang like drums all around the world.

I wish I could play for Sheffield United
And run like David Beckham.

**Kieran Clarke  (8)**
Beck Primary School


# Secret Wishes

I wish I could see a chocolate fountain outside.

I wish I had a chocolate house
Made out of Dairy Milk.

I wish I could have a bike
As fast as a motorbike.

**Niall Martin  (9)**
Beck Primary School

# Fun In Foundation!

Sleeping guinea pigs all cosy and warm in the hutch.
Cheeky children laughing like cheeky monkeys.
Children painting together and painting themselves
In the fun foundation yard.
Children hiding in the grass playing hide-and-seek.
The little children hiding under the window and springing
On the people working hard.
Cheeky pram rolling down the hill into the sunshine
And then the children chasing after the pram.

**Abbie Ramsay  (8)**
**Beck Primary School**


# The Lion

The lion is a golden ball of fire
Burning the savannah down.

He has an amber jewel shredding a horse
With his blood-filled daggers.

He has red jewels staring at his prey.

He has deadly razor blades ripping his enemy.

He has a firework coming out of his jaw.

**Brendan Menday  (9)**
**Beck Primary School**


# The Lion

He has paws like stabbing daggers
He has eyes as hot as laser beams
He has claws like shades
He is as fast as a flying bird
He has a heart like diamonds
He has a noise making the Earth shake.

**Amy Dexter  (9)**
**Beck Primary School**

# The Cheetah Dog

The dog is a colossal cheetah
Zooming through the plants.

He has precious brown jewels
Glistening in the bright sunlight.

He has a soft fluffy brush
Sweeping dust from the floor.

He has smooth black cushions
Resting on a blanket.

He has a warm winter coat
Protecting him from the freezing cold.

He has a deep annoying car horn in his throat
Echoing around the enormous room.

**Keziah Saunders  (9)**
**Beck Primary School**


# The Lion

The lion is a fluffy ball of wool
Fighting fresh green grass every day.

He has amber gems sparkling
Glistening in the midnight sky.

He has fresh white milk teeth
Beaming in the sun.

He has a tickling brush
Swaying through the grass.

He has glistening shining diamonds
That are blue and brown.

**Charlotte Smart  (10)**
**Beck Primary School**

# Richard Fryer

Richard Fryer
Richard Fryer
Turned into a mustard tyre.

Mustard tyre
Mustard tyre
Round and round Richard Fryer.

Richard Fryer
Richard Fryer
Jumped into a tumble dryer.

Tumble dryer
Tumble dryer
Up and down Richard Fryer.

Richard Fryer
Richard Fryer
Looked like a liar.

A liar
A liar
Richard Fryer was as thin as a wire.

**Ronan Hutton  (7)**
**Beck Primary School**


# Richard Fryer

Richard Fryer
Richard Fryer
Stuck his head in a tumble dryer.

Tumble dryer
Tumble dryer
Hot was Mr Fryer.

Mr Fryer
Mr Fryer
Set on fire.

**Kieran Ward  (7)**
**Beck Primary School**

# Mr Ducher

Mr Ducher
Mr Ducher
Is such a sucker.

Mr Sucker
Mr Sucker
Is such a looker.

Mr Looker
Mr Looker
Put his head in a cooker.

Mr Cooker
Mr Cooker
He is not such a looker.

**Kimberley Tickhill  (7)**
**Beck Primary School**


# Richard Fryer

Richard Fryer
Richard Fryer
Stuck his feet in a tumble dryer.

Tumble dryer
Tumble dryer
Made a mess of Richard Fryer.

Richard Fryer
Richard Fryer
Got some more feet made out of wire.

**Katie Sheppard  (7)**
**Beck Primary School**

## Natasha Green

Natasha Green
Natasha Green
Stuck her head in a washing machine.

Washing machine
Washing machine
She got her head stuck in a washing machine.

Washing machine
Washing machine
Round and round Natasha Green.

**Chloe Middleton  (7)**
**Beck Primary School**


## Kelly Pettle

Kelly Pettle
Kelly Pettle
She touched
An electric kettle.

Electric kettle
Electric kettle
It burnt Kelly Pettle.

**Annalise Lilley  ((7)**
**Beck Primary School**


## Helen Stamp

Helen Stamp
Helen Stamp
Put her head on a table lamp.

Table lamp
Table lamp
Last we saw of Helen Stamp.

**Jamie Mayfield  (7)**
**Beck Primary School**

# The Funky Monkey

The monkey is a colossal hairy coconut
Hanging from a banana tree.

He has brunette spikes
Attracting small cheeky fleas.

He has furless pots
Wriggling when he laughs.

He has a soft long stick
Stretching out of his body.

**Abby Turner  (9)**
**Beck Primary School**


# Bethany Pettle

Bethany Pettle
Bethany Pettle
Stuck her hand on an electric kettle.

Electric kettle
Electric kettle
That was the end of Bethany Pettle.

**Callum Taylor  (7)**
**Beck Primary School**


# Mr Wire

Mr Wire
Mr Wire
Had a ride in a tumble dryer.

Tumble dryer
Tumble dryer
He tumbled out poor Mr Wire.

**Joshua Mettam  (7)**
**Beck Primary School**

# Mr Ryan

Mr Ryan
Mr Ryan
Burns himself with an iron.

Steam iron
Steam iron
Falls down on a lion.

Mad lion
Mad lion
Gets attacked by Mr Ryan.

Mr Ryan
Mr Ryan
Gets eaten by a lion.

Hungry lion
Hungry lion
Likes Mr Ryan.

**Jake Mackay  (7)**
**Beck Primary School**


# Mr Wizer

Mr Wizer
Mr Wizer
Stuck his head in a fridge freezer

Fridge freezer
Fridge freezer
Froze the hand of silly Wizer.

Silly Wizer
Silly Wizer
Iced to death in an ice freezer.

**Emily Barnett  (7)**
**Beck Primary School**

# David Stamp

David Stamp
David Stamp
Put his hand on a table lamp.

Table lamp
Table lamp
Don't leave it on a ramp.

Jake Stamp
Jake Stamp
Sat on a bed lamp.

Bed lamp
Bed lamp
I went to bed on a Saturday night.

**Demi Abbott  (7)**
Beck Primary School


# Elisabeth Wire

Elisabeth Wire
Elisabeth Wire
Sets on fire in a tumble dryer.

Tumble dryer
Tumble dryer
Elisabeth Wire sees a liar.

Sees a liar
Sees a liar
Dried to death in a tumble dryer.

Moral: Children don't end up like little Miss Wire.

**Amira Blake  (7)**
Beck Primary School

## Luke Kayer

Luke Kayer
Luke Kayer
Sat on a CD player.

CD player
CD player
That was the last of Luke Kayer.

Taylor Wire
Taylor Wire
Went to catch some fire.

Hot fire
Hot fire
Taylor Wire couldn't catch some fire.

**Bethany Bailey  (7)**
**Beck Primary School**


## James Seazer

James Seazer
James Seazer
Stuck his head in a fridge freezer.

Fridge freezer
Fridge freezer
Colder colder James Seazer.

David Leaner
David Leaner
Took a ride on a vacuum cleaner.

Vacuum cleaner
Vacuum cleaner
Faster, faster David Leaner.

**Luke Bailey  (7)**
**Beck Primary School**

# The Lion

The lion is an animal hunter
Hunting day and night.

He has a chocolate fountain
Making prints wherever he goes.

He has blood-filled needles
Giving people injections.

He has red tears
After chewing something nice.

He has golden wheels
Speeding for his prey.

He is treacle pudding
Pouring down on the ground.

He has shiny daggers
Scraping people to the bone.

**Katie Flanagan  (9)**
**Beck Primary School**


# Rosie Petel

Rosie Petel
Rosie Petel
Burnt her head on a boiling kettle.

Boiling kettle
Boiling kettle
Made a mess of Rosie Petel.

Rosie Petel
Rosie Petel
Got a new arm made of metal.

**Paige Brough, Aaron Knights, Jamie Slater,**
**Kelsey Jarvis & Jade Charlton  (7)**
**Beck Primary School**

# Eight Spiders

Venomous crawler
Egg cuddler
Web spinner
Fly catcher
Bath-side prowler
Speedy rider
Deadly thinker
Blood drinker.

**Lauren Wheeler (10)**
**Beck Primary School**


# Eight Cats

Heart stealer
Cuddle lover
Wool player
String puller
Sofa scratcher
House racer
Vase breaker
Ball sleeper.

**Joe Rodgers (10)**
**Beck Primary School**


# Dolphin

Human lover
Fish eater
Champion diver
Life saver
Breath holder
Speedy jumper
Cheeky joker
Nosey poker.

**Hayley German (10)**
**Beck Primary School**

# The Lion

He is a huge ball of fire
Hunting for his prey.

He has sharpened daggers
Ripping the enemies' flesh.

He has claws like needles
Digging for a deadly animal.

His power is fast as a speed demon
Running as fast as he can.

**Kane Taylor  (9)**
Beck Primary School


# The Lion

The lion is a huge ball of fire
Rolling through the golden-brown savannah.

He has amber jewels
Sparkling like a golden medal.

He has powerful daggers
Shredding his pieces.

He has silver blood-covered needles.

**Sherridan Green  (9)**
Beok Primary School


# Stars

Shining brighter
Boat guider
Everyone's lover
Yellow lighter
Pointy pointer
Hovering higher
Sparkling brighter.

**Laura Pentkethman  (11)**
Beck Primary School

# The Lion

The lion is a huge ball of fire
Rolling through the golden brown savannah.

He has powerful daggers
Shredding his prey to pieces.

He has amber jewels
Sparkling like a golden medal.

He has silver blood-covered needles
Glistening in the sky.

**Ryan Banks  (9)**
**Beck Primary School**


# The Lion

The lion is like a running car
Rolling through the long green grass
He has powerful shredding knives
Digging his knives through his prey.

He has glistening jewels
Sparkling like the lightning in the dark sky
He has needles catching his prey
Sewing through meaty zebras.

**Paul Callaghan  (9)**
**Beck Primary School**


# The Fire-Breathing Lion

The lion is a colossal ball of fire burning down
The forest until it is bare.

He has a grassy coat swaying in the wind.

He has bloody swords after killing his prey.

He is a motor demon whizzing through the forests
Setting fires all over.

**Blake Wilson  (10)**
**Beck Primary School**

# The Lion

The lion has colossal piercing, blood-filled daggers
Shredding his prey to the very last bone.

He has glistening, glowing gems
Shining radiantly in the midnight sky.

He has terribly sharp needles
Injecting people with his fierce blood.

He is a motorbike
Zooming at 300 miles per hour.

**Alex Westney (9)**
**Beck Primary School**

# The Lion

The lion is a huge ball of fire
Rolling through the golden-brown savannah.

He has powerful daggers
Shredding his prey to pieces.

He has amber jewels
Sparkling like a golden medal.

He has silver blood-covered needles
Ripping people.

**Sophie Wilson (9)**
**Beck Primary School**

# David Meaner

David Meaner
David Meaner
Hid in the vacuum cleaner.

Vacuum cleaner
Vacuum cleaner
That's the last of David Meaner.

**Louise Pearce (8)**
**Beck Primary School**

# Move About Monkey

The monkey is a colossal bundle of trouble
Roaming a viney banana tree.

He has huge bare pots
Warming up cheeky disgusting fleas.

He has a bristly jumper
Sitting on top of his body.

He has a tall curvy piece of flexible string
Holding on for dear life.

He has tiny sharp pencils
Grabbing onto some fruit.

**Kelsey Hallam (9)**
**Beck Primary School**


# Monkey

The monkey is cold blooded
Swinging from tree to tree.

He has amber jewels
Sparkling in the night sky.

He has a soft silky blanket
Covering him from the deadly dangers.

He has a toilet brush
Bristling through the leaves.

He has enormous pots
Listening to devastating disasters.

**Anees Botham (9)**
**Beck Primary School**

*Young Writers - Little Laureates Poems From South Yorkshire*

# Junk In Our Trunks

Give us stick insects some proper food!
We don't really like privet and leaves!
We like burgers, hot dogs, ice cream,
Jaffa cakes, Mars bars,
Strawberry creams, chocolate cake,
Whatever we can take!
Pizza, chips,
Coke, crisps.

So don't think we love leaves and bushes,
They make us dizzy and have crazy flushes.
So don't make us have a funny turn,
You really, really need to learn,
We like junk,
In our trunks.

So don't forget it!

**Daisy Fenton  (10)**
**Dore Primary School**


# How Do You Feel?

The sea is a crazy man,
He lives in big, black rocks.
Fierce, vicious, brave and aggressive,
He's a mean, green fighting machine.

You can taste the sickness,
You can see the sickness,
You smell the sickness,
You can hear the boats whizzing by.
You feel like you want to start dancing with the wild beast!

**Sheldon Leigh Hirst  (10)**
**Holy Cross Deanery Primary School**

## The Soothing Stream

A stream is a relaxing beautiful calm place,
Enchanting, refreshing and soothing.
It drips and drops against the dazzling dancing walls.
It is like a peaceful, meandering park.
The river is like a marvellous dream.

**Lisa Wilcock (10)**
**Holy Cross Deanery Primary School**


## The River

A river is a crashing noise.
A burst of water.
Dazzling, dazzles like lightning.
It is like a scary storm.
The noise is thunderous in my ears.

**Lewis Kelk (10)**
**Holy Cross Deanery Primary School**


## The Water Monster

The waterfall is a violent and aggressive monster.
Lethal, barbaric, vicious.
It jumps on the rough rocks, crashing down.
The waterfall is a raging monster.

**Chloe Bent (9)**
**Holy Cross Deanery Primary School**


## The Swordsman

The river flows aggressively just like a swordsman.
It bangs against the banged up river bank.
Then it comes to a feathery, heavenly stop.

**Liam Woodcock (10)**
**Holy Cross Deanery Primary School**

# The Sea

The sea is a dangerous water
Very vicious, violent, shark, nasty.
It's smashing, crashing, bashing,
It breathes in and out louder than an animal
And the waves go bashing into the air.

**Ellis Higgins (10)**
Holy Cross Deanery Primary School

# The Beautiful Waterfall

A waterfall is beautiful, water crashing on the rocks.
White spray goes everywhere, slamming all over in an angry rage!
Fierce, rough, fearful.
The water ripples all over.

**Ciara Owen (11)**
Holy Cross Deanery Primary School

# The Sea

The sea is like an angry dog, fierce, vicious, ferocious.
It smashes into a spiky rock.
It is like a vile beast.
It breathes nearly like it has asthma.

**Brandon Semmens (11)**
Holy Cross Deanery Primary School

# The Relaxed River

A river flows smoothly down the bank as slow as a snail.
Sparkling, beautiful, dazzling.
It is a baby in a cot.
It is a calm and caring crystal-blue diamond.

**Curtis Firth (10)**
Holy Cross Deanery Primary School

# The Vicious Waterfall

As quick as a lightning bolt, it shatters the rigid rocks.
Berserk, brutal, lethal.
Crashing, smashing on the riverbank.
The waterfall wrapping round the colourful fish.

As calm as God it flows down the river.
Beloved, sedate, unstoppable, gently moving on,
Dancing on the riverbank.
Sparkling, flashing in the sun as it winds its way to the sea.

**Brent Barraclough  (10)**
**Holy Cross Deanery Primary School**


# The Raging Flood

A flood flashes through the streets.
Destroying things in its path.
As people hurry the flood has still got its fury.
Lethal, vicious and mad.
Nobody can stop him.
He soars and roars into homes
Who can stop him nobody knows . . .

**Ellie Clarkson  (10)**
**Holy Cross Deanery Primary School**


# A Wonderful Waterfall

As calm as a cat,
Softly, peacefully and dazzling.
The waterfall is a cool place,
You can feel all of the senses,
Touch, hear, smell, taste and see.
You can see the sun bouncing off the waterfall.
Amazing, glittering and beautiful.

**Brittany Callaghan  (9)**
**Holy Cross Deanery Primary School**

# A Magical River

A river is a calm, warm, living thing.
Silent, magical, enchanting.
It flows silently without a sound.
Small friendly fish swimming their way across the dazzling river.
As it glitters in the sun everyone sees how beautiful it is.
It is proud to be a river.

**Rebekah Morley (9)**
Holy Cross Deanery Primary School


# Sea

The sea is a ferocious giant.
Violent, powerful, barbaric.
It crashes, bashes against the raggy rocks.
It's like a vile beast.

**Chloe Harpin (10)**
Holy Cross Deanery Primary School


# The Rocky Sea

The sea is a vicious, giant man.
Angry, thunderous and aggressive.
It crashes and smashes against the rocky cliff.
It is like an enormous wrestler.

**Liam Lindley (11)**
Holy Cross Deanery Primary School


# The Monster Sea

It is angry, wrestling with the razor-like vile, vicious giant.
It crashes and smashes into the rocks punishing them.
It stomps all over the rocks, breaking down the rocks.

**Reece Hamer (10)**
Holy Cross Deanery Primary School

# I Should Like To Paint

I should like to paint the sound of
A hyena cackling while pacing the deserted plains,
The thud of a drum banging in regular rhythm
And the mighty roar of a bulky bear.

I should like to paint the touch of
Pliable, furry pearl-white snow falling like a feather,
The touch of a dog snoozing into a pillow,
The feel of a tomato squelching in your hand.

I should like to paint the smell of
Scented candles, their aroma drifting in the polluted air,
The smell of aftershave wafting in the air,
The aroma of lavender floating around me.

I should like to paint the taste of
Warm, slurpy hot chocolate gushing into my stomach,
Yummy ice cream trickling down my throat,
The taste of scrumptious chips chomping in my mouth.

I should like to paint the sight of
A chloric ant heaving food upon his puny back stumbling then
                                    regaining his balance,
A F1 Ferrari swinging towards the finish,
The sight of neon lights flickering in the night.

**Daniel Thorpe (9)**
**Limpsfield Junior School**


# Spider

Amber stars glowing in the coal-black sky
Swiftly dancing on sharp sensitive claws
Stabbing the air
As she waves her sparkling snowflake.

**Charlotte Slack (10)**
**Limpsfield Junior School**

# The Magic Box

*(Based on 'Magic Box' by Kit Wright)*

I will put in my box . . .
The roaring fire from a supersonic rocket,
A chocolate shop that's like a smooth soft bed that melts on my
tongue,
The fragrance of the sizzling sausages from the delicious hot dogs
At my fantasy fairground.

I will put in my box . . .
The silky touch of the feathery horse trotting on a creamy racecourse,
The softness of the fierce fire burning from the ferocious dragon,
The salty sea waving to the surfers on the sandy shore.

My box is fashioned from everlasting ice cream with the chocolatiest
chips,
The lid is made of sickly chocolate chip cookies,
Hidden in the corners are David Beckham stickers,
And the hinges are made from the doors of the fastest cars in the
universe.

I will play Fantasy Football with Steven Gerrard and David Beckham
in my box,
Then we would all go to a paradise and swim with the bluest whales.

**Liam Ashton (7)**
**Limpsfield Junior School**


# The Winter Day

The foggy tranquil sky surrounded everything lifelessly.

As the bristly, spiky branch hovered lurching like a slim hand
Reaching out.

Bitter sprinkle of snow settled on the trees
Standing as still as fearless soldiers.

Swaying snow-covered trees stayed captured in the winter's breeze.

Lonely mountains were imprisoned in the freezing day.

**Sophie Hurt (10)**
**Limpsfield Junior School**

# I Should Like To Paint!

I should like to paint the sound of
Rustling leaves angrily flowing in the night sky,
The wind whistling through my ears
And the trickling of water whooshing down a cliff.

I should like to paint the touch of
Soft grains of sand tumbling through my fingers,
Wrinkly tree bark smiling at me while I climb its branches
And my golden hair waving in my face as I run down the street.

I should like to paint the taste of
Sour apples, anxious while I bite my teeth through them,
Crispy pancakes with golden syrup being poured on top
And the creamy warmth of hot chocolate being stirred in a pot.

I should like to paint the smell of
Intoxicating perfume being squirted onto my soft body,
Scarlet red flowers being pollinated by bees
And the salty smell of the tide crashing in.

I should like to paint the sight of
Fireworks banging in the night sky while I'm in bed,
The man on the moon saying 'hello'
And the sparkling sight of the sunset while I stand on the horizon.

**Emily-Rose Bower  (9)**
**Limpsfield Junior School**


# Spider

Gold, black leopard skin
Dancing on crooked daggers
Flinching from side to side
Delicately weaving an elegant snowflake
With fine laced thread.

**Lucas Cawthorne**
**Limpsfield Junior School**

# I Should Like To Paint

I should like to paint the taste of
A crispy chicken burger exploding with flavour,
Creamy hot chocolate drifting like a stream of happiness,
Delicious, de-caf coffee swirling like a whirlpool of desire.

I should like to paint the sound of
A helicopter whirring its propellers rapidly,
A hairy guinea pig crying uncontrollably,
The sound of silence in the cool night air.

I should like to paint the smell of
Petrol drifting through the air,
Fresh air travelling everywhere,
Barbecued burgers making me so hungry as they
Cook over the untouchable heat.

I should like to paint the touch of
Clay squelching in my hands as I mould it into a cup-like shape.
Smooth, solid marble of a new gravestone lying in a cold, silent
graveyard.

**Josh Parker (10)**
Limpsfield Junior School


# I Should Like To Paint

I should like to paint the sound of . . .
A beautiful medium brown and scarlet-red, robin
Chanting its song beautifully on a frosty morning,
A stream trickling down a pathway of smooth
Spiky rocks into a dark misty cavern.

I should like to paint the smell of . . .
Lots of crispy burning wood on a misty, cold Bonfire Night,
Carbonated petrol in a petrol station, full of humming cars.

I should like to paint the taste of . . .
Oily, golden chips with fresh fish and shiny, crispy batter,
Hot, steaming chocolate gushing down my open throat,
Like a surging brown waterfall.

**Jack Kazmierkiewicz (9)**
Limpsfield Junior School

# I Should Like To Paint!

I should like to paint the smell of . . .
A freshly blown candle upon an iced birthday cake,
Lavender blowing in the breeze creating its own unique perfume,
Pulling up into a petrol station with the distinct smell of petrol
Whirring around me.

I should like to paint the sound of . . .
Crisp white snow with freshly formed footprints in midwinter,
Whooshing and whirling waterfalls trickling into the huge, still lakes
With jagged rocks thrown in, concentric circles slowly forming,
Crinkling, crackling wrapping paper in all different colours and sizes,
Being ripped into minute pieces.

I should like to paint the taste of . . .
Pasta smothered in succulent tomato puree smelling like a
                                                    heavenly dream,
Melting, creamy chocolate sailing like a cruiser down my rough,
                                                    bumpy throat,
Fluffy pink candyfloss dissolving in my mouth with a little morsel left
                                                    on my chin.

I should like to paint the sight of . . .
A relaxing, calming sunset, descending on the gentle breeze while
Skies turn pinks, purples and oranges,
Tears of the chocolate fountain flowing into the gleaming tray at the
Bottom creating a tempting sight,
Colossal, powerful horses jumping tall hurdles using all their strength
                                                    and muscles.

I should like to paint the touch of . . .
Smooth, cold silk used on my pillow cover soothing me to sleep,
Soft, fluffy teddy bears that I cuddle as if they are my best
                                                    friends forever,
Petite, furry rabbits shaking on my knee with their triangular noses
                                                    twitching rapidly.

**Megan Oliver  (9)**
**Limpsfield Junior School**

# I Should Like To Paint

I should like to paint the sound of
A flock of birds endlessly singing in the morning breeze,
The calm sea sweeping ahead through a shell,
Sizzling fire cackling hysterically on a barbecue.

I should like to paint the taste of
A scrumptious stick of rock releasing its sweet taste,
As I crunch it at the seaside,
Sticky candyfloss as it melts in my mouth at the seaside,
Chocolate cake oozing with icing and topped with a cherry.

I should like to paint the smell of fruity shampoos and conditioners
Smothered on my hair,
The sightless salt in the sea at the seaside,
Melting chocolate bursting with flavour in the oven.

I should like to paint the touch of
The soft silk of a dress circling my hands,
The furry, velvety skin of a peach rubbing against my cheek,
Babies' sleek skin as smooth as silk.

I should like to paint the look of
Shooting stars soaring through the night sky,
Frightening fireworks erupting in an instant,
The flowing waves crashing into the rocks at the shore.

**Shaiyan Moss  (11)**
**Limpsfield Junior School**

# The Magic Box
*(Based on 'Magic Box' by Kit Wright)*

I will put in the box . . .
The loud engines from a bright red motorbike racing along the track,
The taste of sweet Galaxy chocolate bar with delicious caramel milk,
The fragrance of sweet candyfloss crawling up my nose.

I will put in the box . . .
The wet touch of the enormous blue sea whilst dashing smoothly
                                        into the seashore,
The night stars sparkling crystal clear down on every single person
                                        on Earth.

My box is fashioned from
Sparkling glass covered in star sticks with a tortoise shell for the lid.
There are secret cameras in the corners with my dad's toes for
                                        the hinges.

I will climb enormous rocks beside the sea, where the high waves
                                        dash into the seashore.

**Daniel Whiteman  (7)**
**Limpsfield Junior School**


# The Magic Box
*(Based on 'Magic Box' by Kit Wright)*

I will put in my box . . .
The thundering engines from the bright red motorbike
The delicious chocolate cake that melts on the tip of my tongue
The scent of paint walking up my nose.

I will put in my box . . .
The invisible touch of a baseball waving on my hand,
Gold and silver fire from a dragon's nostrils.

My box is fashioned from silver fire and my lid is made from gold
Stickers and my corners are made of secret spells
My hinges are made from football stickers of Paddy Kenny.

I will jump in my box all night and all day
Eating fish and chips.

**Cameron Hizam  (8)**
**Limpsfield Junior School**

# I Should Like To Paint . . .

I should like to paint the sound of
The teacher exclaiming, 'It's hometime,' on the last day of school
The crackle of bacon blistering in a frying pan
A car crying to life in the midnight darkness.

I should like to paint the taste of
A fresh fried fish on a Friday night,
Oven-fresh cakes oozing chocolate like a geyser,
Home-made Sunday lunch made by my
Naughty nan.

I should like to paint the smell of
An aromatic apple blossom floating off a tree,
New roses in the rarely kept clean garden
Fresh when laid out on the bed.

I should like to paint the touch of
My rough rascally dog's fur in my house
The crisp touch of autumn leaves,
The squelch of mud underfoot.

I should like to paint the look of
My dog racing to me after a day at school
Burgers flipping in the air
My TV jumping to life at the touch of a button.

I should like to capture
The secret of a cartoon flickering on TV
The light from the mystical magical moon
The glow of a child's smile on Christmas Day.

**James Bonnett (10)**
**Limpsfield Junior School**

# The Magic Box

*(Based on 'Magic Box' by Kit Wright)*

I will put in the box . . .
A chocolate fountain dripping into a yummy chocolate lake
Melting on the tip of my tongue.
A cherry candyfloss with blueberries melting like a cake.
A fragrance of perfume walking up my nose smelling of colourful
strawberries.

I will put in the box . . .
The touch of the fluttering soft multicoloured butterflies
A sparkly dress that feels like a blue diamond.

My box is fashioned from sparkly diamonds glittering like the blue sea
The lid is made from a gorgeous strawberry milkshake.
My hinges are golden hair from a beautiful princess.

I will swim all day in the bluest pool and fall on the cleanest softest
sand.

In the corners there is the smallest most beautiful pixie
That gives me whatever I wish for.

In my box
Are colourful fireworks whooshing up and popping into little specks.

**Dannielle Snee (8)**
**Limpsfield Junior School**

# The Magic Box

*(Based on 'Magic Box' by Kit Wright)*

I will put in the box . . .
The melting, crunchy, creamy marshmallow bar that explodes
                                        strawberry flavours.
A cherry-bodied dragon with bluey yellow wings whose fiery breath
Shoots out like burning snowflakes.

I will put in the box . . .
The most delicious chocolate cake that makes me feel like I am flying
Towards a moon made out of sweet Coco Pops.

My box is fashioned from
A witch's sparkling spell.
My lid is fashioned from
Glittering rubies that make my room sparkle
When the clock reaches 8 o'clock.

I will roller blade and eat minty sweets in my box
Then I will cuddle my cute baby brother,
My two big sisters and my best friends Chloe and Dannielle.
If a crazy crocodile wants to eat them, I will turn into
Super Stacey and save them just in time.

**Stacey Mazorodze  (7)**
**Limpsfield Junior School**

# The Magic Box

*(Based on 'Magic Box' by Kit Wright)*

I will put in the box . . .
The strawberry candyfloss that tastes like raspberry ripple
And melts on the tip of my tongue.
A crystal ring that sparkles like a disco ball at a party.

I will put in the box . . .
A sweet smell of chocolatey perfume that goes round my nostrils
all day,
The fluffy touch of a multicoloured silk that creases in the cold
draught.

My box is fashioned from crystals also delicate roses
And a silver enormous ribbon tied on the top.
The lid is made of glamorous diamonds and beautiful charms,
In the corners there are secret cameras hidden in the corners.
My hinges are made of a Mexican parrot's feathers that unlocks
my box.
No one can get into it without my secret key.

I will jump into chocolate world and eat all the chocolate on Thursday.
I will eat white chocolate, but on Sunday, I will jump in and pretend
I am on holiday.

**Chloe Needham (7)**
**Limpsfield Junior School**

# The Magic Box

*(Based on 'Magic Box' by Kit Wright)*

I will put in the box . . .
Melted chocolate dripping like gravy over fresh roast chicken.
A bubbly milkshake that tastes like my dad's cheesy smelly socks
A sweet scent of bluebells.

I will put in the box . . .
The aroma of sizzling lasagne
The invisible touch of salty, soft, candyfloss whooshing through the
window,
Clickety-clack, clack, clack of my dancing shoes tapping in my
bedroom.

My box is fashioned from delicate crystals and roses with steel and
glitter,
The lid is made of glittery rubies and snow that is like sand
My corners have magical crystals that when you say 'I wish', it comes
true,
The hinges are made of the fins of a dolphin.

I will ice skate all night and all day till I get tired
And eat luscious, party food, watching terrifying films.

**Hollie Bower  (8)**
**Limpsfield Junior School**

# The Magic Box
*(Based on 'Magic Box' by Kit Wright)*

I will put in my box . . .
A drip-drop of chocolate gravy of a golden chicken,
Some juicy sweets that feel like getting into my warm bed
The fragrance of fish because it's brain food.

I will put in my box . . .
The invisible touch of candyfloss waving and whooshing in the wind.
A magnificent butterfly with its red and silky wings flapping in the
gracious garden.

My box is fashioned from everlasting ice cream.
My lid is made of pinky candyfloss.
My corners are made of delicate roses.

I would like to skate all day and night in my box,
And dive into a gorgeous swimming pool.

**Caitlin Moore (7)**
**Limpsfield Junior School**


# The Magic Box
*(Based on 'Magic Box' by Kit Wright)*

I will put in the box . . .
The drip drop of chocolate falling down a massive fountain.
Sniff scented flowers floating on my tongue.

I will put in the box . . .
Sweet candyfloss floating on my mouth.

My box is fashioned from shiny rings and golden necklaces.
The lid is made of golden treasures and in the corner there is
golden money.

The hinges smell of my dad's smelly sweaty feet.

I will sing Bratz Rock Angels' song,
All day and night,
And while I sing I'll feel delighted and glad.

**Jomana Mare (7)**
**Limpsfield Junior School**

# The Magic Box

*(Based on 'Magic Box' by Kit Wright)*

I will put in the box . . .
The soft touch of invisible clouds,
The melted caramel that drops onto my pink long tongue
The sparkle of fireworks shooting up into the air.

I will put in the box . . .
The clippety-clop of my dancing shoes,
A milky caramel chocolate bar that feels like pillows on my tongue
I can smell the sweet deodorant from my mum's bedroom.

I will put in the box . . .
The drip drop of chocolate of a colourful chocolate fountain
The chocolate caramel dropping from us above in Heaven.

My box is fashioned from sizzling crystals and diamonds.
The lid is made of glittering charms
My corners have magical wings and the hinges are made of the fins
of a dolphin
I will dance in my box all day until the sun goes down.

**Nicole Lindsay  (8)**
**Limpsfield Junior School**


# My Magic Box

*(Based on 'Magic Box' by Kit Wright)*

I will put in my box . . .
A glittery star from the washing waves from the seven seas,
An icy white waterfall from the magical Atlantic ocean
The smile of Zac Efron's cute face
A glossy bit of dragon fire out of a Chinese dragon.

I will put in my box . . .
The cute giggle of my sweet baby Francesca
My best friend's handwriting
The lovely faces of my mum and dad and Olivia
An orange pearl from an amazing clam
The cute face of my cousin Victoria.

**Jessica Beck  (7)**
**Limpsfield Junior School**

# My Magic Box

*(Based on 'Magic Box' by Kit Wright)*

I will put in my box . . .
The first gleaming tooth of a baby
The shiny dust of a fairy
The breath of a fiery dragon in the morning
A million dreams.

I will put in my box . . .
The waves from the seven seas
The glittery stone from the baby of Wales
A shine from a shooting star
A magical kitten from kitten world
A gleaming floating car
A magnificent time machine.

I will put in my box . . .
A silly dancing skeleton
A leaf from a season
A gleaming shooting star
A supersonic motorbike
A hair from a ferocious lion
A cute puppy.

**Bryn Wainwright  (7)**
**Limpsfield Junior School**

# My Magic Box

*(Based on 'Magic Box' by Kit Wright)*

I will put in my box . . .
A magical window that's golden.
A pebble from the seven seas.
The first tooth from a baby.
The fantastic Pirates of the Caribbean.
A magical star from the Atlantic ocean
An eagle with black scary feathers
The heart of Davy Jones.

I will put in my box . . .
Some fire from an American dragon
A tree with stars on
A mask of Tutankhamun
A hot pancake with cheese on
A relaxing bath with candles.

**Liam Claricoats (7)**
**Limpsfield Junior School**


# Beowulf's Dragon

The cave was dripping with the rain
The wind was whistling in the night's darkness
Snoring as loud as the waves
Its breath was as cold as ice
Enormous turquoise scales
Red spikes on its spine
Its claws were as sharp as a knight's sword
As lonely as a prisoner in a cell.

Frost on its body
Sabotaged wings, bleeding scabs
Breathtaking gold
Red rubies, shimmering diamonds
A slave managed to grab some gold
The dragon's cat's eyes looked around like a dog
It flew up into the air puffing on that winter night.

**Bethany McCall (8)**
**Montagu Junior School**

# Beowulf's Dragon

It was as cold as the coldest winter,
The wind was as angry as annoyed swarm of wasps.
The cave had stalagmites as sharp as needles made of rock.
Inside it was shadowy as Alton Towers at night when all the lights
go out.

The dragon was as lonely as an abandoned dog.
He was petrifying enough to stop your heart,
As self-centred as Goliath,
With breath as hot as an incinerator;
He reeked like ninety-year-old milk mixed with bug-infested, rotten
fungi.

He had scales as slippy as ice.
The gold was breathtaking and so, so gorgeous
Treasure blinding with a deathening sparkle.
Suddenly the dragon loudly yawned and stretched
He saw the gold was gone . . .

**Joshua Troop (9)**
Montagu Junior School


# Beowulf's Dragon

It was raining hard.
The dragon slept in its gold-filled cave
Every time it breathed it roared.
It was a gloomy dark and cold night.
The air was as cold as the Arctic.
The jagged teeth were razor-sharp,
Its breath smelt dreadful like rotten food.
It had scabs all over its back.
Its roar was so loud you could hear it from 200 miles away.

The treasure was as smooth as a block of ice
It was as shiny as moonlight beaming down on the ground
Green goblets, ruby-red glimmering diamonds
A slave managed to grab some without the dragon seeing
When the dragon woke up and noticed its treasure was gone.

**Danielle Poole (8)**
Montagu Junior School

# Beowulf's Dragon

The sky was so dark.
The lightning flashed.
The rain was so fast.
It sounded like hailstones.
It was cold as ice.
Enormous stones trapped around you.
The cave was hideous and you couldn't see all of your body.
The dragon's breath was threatening, like an orangey red beam
                                                    of light.
The dragon's head was as big as a treetop.
The body of the dragon was as massive as a witch's spooky tower
His tail was as long as a motorway.
His treasure was like gleaming white snow.
The dragon woke up stretching as long as he could.
He looked around with his eyes sparkling like red rubies.

**Darren Pearson  (9)**
**Montagu Junior School**


# Beowulf's Dragon

On a gloomy, dark, scary night.
Bushes rattled in the freezing breeze.
Lightning flashed in the heavy rain.
Bare trees shook like a volcano about to burst.
With boiling hot lava slithering down it.
In a gigantic cave a lazy dragon had slept
For a thousand winters.
He had razor-sharp teeth that felt as pointy as
Sixty pocket knives in your face.
Its breath smelt as bad as a stinky swamp.
It snored as loud as two knights charging at each other with spears.
He was as lonely as an abandoned house.

Later on that night a sly slave crept into the foul and filthy cave.
The slave grabbed a handful of gold
And ran as fast as his legs could carry him.

**Callum Bater  (8)**
**Montagu Junior School**

# Beowulf's Dragon

The weather was as cold as ice.
It was pitch-black outside.
The dragon's teeth were as sharp as a chainsaw;
His breath was as smelly as a block of rotten cheese.
His nose was longer than a carving knife.
His body was as terrifying as a stone wall crashing to the ground.
His scales were as prickly as crocodile's teeth.
His horns were sharper than 1000 knives.
The scales were as green as flower stalks.
The dragon's teeth were as brown as a tree trunk.
His breath was even worse than a swamp.
The treasure shimmered in the hard chest
The gold sparkled in the cold night.
The gold glittered more than a bright silver knife.

**Emily Hargreaves  (8)**
**Montagu Junior School**


# Beowulf's Dragon

It was as cold as ice.
Its claws were as sharp as a chainsaw.
Its horns were as big as a sycamore tree.
Its eyes were as dark as caves.
Its tail was as long as six trees.

Its scales were as multicoloured as leaves in summer
The dragon's fire was as hot as trees burning in the wind.
The dragon was hiding thousands of jewel like
The rubies were as red as strawberries.
Also the sapphires were as blue as blueberries.
Beowulf saw the creepy rotten people lying on the floor.
The floor was as cold as an ice skating ring.

**Shelby Gilliver  (8)**
**Montagu Junior School**

# Beowulf's Dragon

His teeth are as sharp and as ferocious as a tiger.
His wings are dirtier than a 100-year-old
Wizard who hasn't had a bath for weeks.
His feet are as smelly as one million
Rotting mushrooms.
His breath is as hot as the sun.
His claws are as sharp as shark's teeth.
His scales are bright pink.
His tail is as pointy and as strong as the
Biggest wrestler that could kill me.
His gold is like a shimmering waterfall
Pouring down the rocks.
His glowing ruby gems lit up the cave
All in red.
The dragon was waking up as slow as can be.
He opened one eye then he opened the other,
And he roared really loud.

**Cara Bennett (8)**
**Montagu Junior School**

# Beowulf's Dragon

His home was pitch-black and cold as could be.
His wings were terrifying
Underneath they were green and slimy.
Inside gold glimmered like the beaming sun.
The dragon's teeth were longer than chainsaws.
The dragon roared so loudly he made a tumbling avalanche.
The deep snow crashed down.
His fire was so bright it could blind people.
His fire melted the snow quicker than a blink of an eye.
The dragon's claws were really sharp and scary.
His cave was so bright you could see it from as far away.
The man ran as fast as his legs would.

**George Goodinson (8)**
**Montagu Junior School**

# Wonderful Seasons

*Winter*
Pure white snow trickling down to the floor,
Snow White is dancing with the snowflakes,
Roofs are covered in white crystal shapes,
And you'd better wrap up in warm clothes kids!

*Autumn*
Green leaves turn to reds, oranges, browns and yellows,
Trees soon turn bare,
Leaves turn crispy and curly,
And gently leaves are falling to the floor.

*Summer*
The warm sunshine is here,
Kids are out in the swimming pool,
Parents are sunbathing (*boring!*)
And everyone is having *fun!*

*Spring*
Flowers are growing in gardens,
Beautiful colours cover farm fields,
Fruit and veg are being picked by children,
For a family feast.

**Shannon Ferguson-Corrie (10)**
**Montagu Junior School**

# Beowulf's Dragon

It was as dark as a midnight crow
Cold ice-like floor
Along the stone ridden scorch-marked road
He dashed swiftly
To the stalactite-covered cave
Lay he on the floor
As dawn broke
Horrified as he stood
Facing the rotting bodies
The dragon's claws were like a pile of vampire stakes
His scales as green as a flock of locusts
His nose squished up as the smell of bodies
Crawled up his nose.

The dragon looked like it was shimmering
But it was the shining gold's reflection
A red jewel gleamed on its victim's shattered head
As the slave dashed swiftly forward
He snatched the jewel
He raced out of the cave
The dragon slowly woke.
His roar was like a thousand boulders crashing down.

**Louis Finney  (9)**
**Montagu Junior School**

# Beowulf's Dragon

His scales were as neat as a fish's,
His tail was as long as a whale,
His teeth was as sharp as a wolf's.
His breath smelt like an apple in a junkyard rotting.
His treasure was as beautiful as a princess's crown,
Shimmering gold gleaming in the dark night,
Pearls as smooth as a velvet gown,
Sapphires blending in with colourful jewels.
His cave was so dark you couldn't see your hand,
Green slimy fungus dripping everywhere,
The dragon sneezed fire and suddenly awoke,
The roar was so loud the ground shook.
Outside his scales froze,
He took a giant stride,
And roared as loud as the sea crashing.

**Laura Gibbons  (8)**
**Montagu Junior School**


# My Massive Rocket

My massive rocket is rusty and grey
Smells like petrol
And needs a spray.

My massive rocket is powered up to go
Straight to the moon
When I'm ready that'll be soon.

Picnics and drinks all in a bag
Come on dog
You big old hag.

My massive rocket has landed on the moon
Goodbye everyone
I'll see you soon.

**Louis Moore  (10)**
**St Joseph's Catholic Primary School, Doncaster**

# Super Striker I'm Going Mad

Runnin' fast
What a blast,
Dodgin' people,
Kickin' people,
Gettin' the ball,
Score a goal,
Gettin' muddy with my buddies
Score the goal in the last ten seconds
Woo! We won,
I win the final gold cup,
I am really a striker,
I'm mad, I think I'm goin' to die,
Doin' break dancin'
Handstands,
Saying booya beat ya to the losin' team
Saying beat ya beat ya oh yeah!

**Sofia Calzini (8)**
**St Joseph's Catholic Primary School, Doncaster**


# David Beckham The Best Striker

Best striker dancin' around
Jumpin' high up and down
Skippin' low, jumpin' high
All dirty
Doesn't care
He's goin' to do it all again *yeah!*
Exit the other door
Go home
Go to bed
Tomorrow is a brand new day.

**Holly Wilson (8)**
**St Joseph's Catholic Primary School, Doncaster**

# I Love The Little Pony!

There is a little pony at the bottom of my garden.
It is frisky and playful,
So much fun for me,
To sit at the fence and watch it,
After I've had my tea!

But no one comes to feed it,
Or make it a nice warm bed.
All those horrible thoughts,
Bounce around my head.

Its coat is thick and matted
Its feet soft and cracked.
It's awfully head-shy
I think it has been smacked!

I love that little pony,
I look after it as if it is mine.
I play with it and love it,
Till after my bedtime!

**Stephanie Gillespie  (10)**
**St Joseph's Catholic Primary School, Doncaster**


# Robinson

Goal savin' rockin' ravin'
Up, down all around
Kickin' far, nearly got a car
Flipper unney just like Rooney
All the time savin' the town
Magic moves, rough Robinson
Slippin' slidin' all day long
All my fans screamin' England
I am super goalie!

**Laurence Anthony  (8)**
**St Joseph's Catholic Primary School, Doncaster**

# The Obstacle Course

At the start there is a pole,
Telling you where to go.
After that a wire net,
Seems like mini Mount Everest.
Over the top they go,
Slowly but surely.

Then over a thin block,
Covering the murky swamp.
One falls in, then gets out,
Covered in the mucky grout.

Climbing up suspended bricks,
Is the next enormous task.
Hanging on a rusty wire,
The adventurers climb upwards.
One reaches the top,
Then helps the others follow.
They've reached the top. They've done it
And in a quick time too.

**Mark Donnelly (10)**
**St Joseph's Catholic Primary School, Doncaster**


# Super Saver Celebrating Keeper

Super saver football waver
I blast the ball high in the sky
It lands in the net and I'm all wet
The lights are flashin' the football players
Are dashin'
We get fouled the crowd goes wild
The ball's on the line and it's nearly half-time
We have a rest then we go back on
We win the game and the cup.

**Callum Godley (8)**
**St Joseph's Catholic Primary School, Doncaster**

# Trees

Trees are like a living human,
They eat, drink and sleep, I think.

They are green, amber, gold, red and brown,
That's the colours of a tree.

They come in all shapes and sizes,
Big, little, tall, small, they're the trees I like.

Old and wrinkly the bark a
Chocolatey brown and mossy!

Trees should be respected,
They help us breathe and grow.

That's what trees are!

**Hannah Duffy (11)**
St Joseph's Catholic Primary School, Doncaster

# The Super Football Match

Super keeper savin' goals, headin'
Them out is his job in goal,
As the goalie he has to jump
Up to the ball to stop it from scorin'
Sometimes he can't stop slidin',
And other times he just keeps fallin' down
Other footballers keep dodgin'
Me and my friends are best at tacklin'
But we are still very good at scorin'
People in the crowd are going mad wavin' hands,
I can hear people celebratin' at home!

**Amy Lynch (9)**
St Joseph's Catholic Primary School, Doncaster

# Fire Fire Fireworks

The fire in the garden is blazing and burning
The smells are bitter the wood is burning
It rustles and snaps
All you hear is *whizz, whoosh* and *screech*
The fireworks exploding, glittering rockets,
Fire crackers, Catherine wheels, bangers and fountains
Colourful, dazzling, ear-splitting shooting stars
Fierce, hissing, popping
Fireworks they never stop.

Hot dogs, burgers, potatoes too
Marshmallows for me and you
Mums, dads and aunties too chatting to me and you
Seeing the fire go out, rubble, earth, iron and wood.

Mum and Dad washing up the dishes
Getting ready for bed
Another day where we had more *fun!*

**Alex Charlesworth  (11)**
**St Joseph's Catholic Primary School, Doncaster**


# Crazy Keeper

He's a super saver, fast mover
High jumper, low diver
Good booter, brill mover
Not a score in sight, it's probably his height
There it goes, who knows
Ten-nil, what a score, ten-nil *I want more!*
What a save, have a rave
Yes we won, I'm proud of you son.

**Declan McMenamin  (8)**
**St Joseph's Catholic Primary School, Doncaster**

# The Super Striker

Super striker runnin' everywhere
Bootin' volleyin' kickin' dodging
Tacklin' and scorin' goals
But the best one of all was
The boot from the halfway line
He's the best scorer of them all
But when he celebrates he is crazy
He flips, he does a handstand and
He does all sorts of things
When he goes to football
It always has been on a rainy day
When the clouds are grey and you can hear
Rumblin' in the sky, flashes of lightning and it is
Always cold, very, very cold so the players
Have to always wear long sleeves, but he will
Never miss because he's got a super hard power kick
The goals he shoots but he's the super striker!
And he says, 'See you later man!'

**Liam Gormley  (8)**
**St Joseph's Catholic Primary School, Doncaster**


# World Winning Striker

I am the world winnin' striker
Bold and good,
You should see what my friends think, they think I'm good.
Rampagin', headbuttin', runnin' around makin' sounds, that's me
The world winnin' striker
Gettin' muddy is a goodie, kickin' and shootin' is my dream,
Winnin' the cup is what I want and I can do it because I am the super
striker
Now that's a little thing about me, that you can sing about with me,
And I am the world winnin' striker! *Yeah!*

**Jasmine West  (8)**
**St Joseph's Catholic Primary School, Doncaster**

# Parrots!

P arrots are so cool
A ren't they so dazzling
R ed, blue and yellow, examples of their colours
R ight or wrong, they are nice to look at
O h they are expensive, but I love them so!
T hey make a lot of racket and speak to you
S o here's the last thing I'm going to tell you
            *Go get one!*

**Lauren Forest (11)**
**St Joseph's Catholic Primary School, Doncaster**


# Striker

Handstandin' goal shootin' what a boot in the hoop
What a goal in a hole,
Best striker arm wavin' kiss throwin' everywhere
Team huggin' from a ball to the goal so they won't fall
Last minute, what a limit so they fit it
Manchester cried because they never lost so it will cost
Today, one-nil
When a footballer is tall in the hall with a ball he can score!

**Alex Godley (8)**
**St Joseph's Catholic Primary School, Doncaster**


# Crazy Strike

Super striker rockin' rollin' fast mover handstandin'
High jumper for a header from their throw,
Laid out good for the striker
*Bang!* he shoots, the commentator says, 'Them boots aren't for
Tappin' they're for smackin'.'
All the fans go wild when he scores,
*Striker!*

**Jordan Saunders (8)**
**St Joseph's Catholic Primary School, Doncaster**

# Limo!

Long and white, gleaming silver glass.
Long fun parties with a friend.
Lively dancing and out of tune karaoke!
At my friend Georgia's party!

Georgia's superstar mum is showing her up,
Glamorous outfits mucked up by sticky sarnies,
Gorgeous hair waving wildly while everybody dances,
At my friend Georgia's party!

Hooray! Hooray! We're out again,
Hummer limo, starry-bright or midnight-black?
Heather, (that's me!) Georgia and her mum,
In my friend Georgia's limo!

**Heather Lukins  (10)**
**St Joseph's Catholic Primary School, Doncaster**


# The Haunted Hotel

The werewolf howling outside.
Professor Frankenstein inventing
In the bleak basement.
Dracula snoring away until midnight.
The wraith slicing 'n' dicing a few guests.
The gremlins spooking a few of them.
The bogeyman haunting the bathroom.
Zombies are on room service.
Phantoms going through walls
And shouting rude things.
It's lots of fun in the Haunted Hotel
I wonder why we have few guests?

**Haydn Ellis  (10)**
**St Joseph's Catholic Primary School, Doncaster**

## Supersaver Celebrating Keeper

What a day
What a play
Big bashes at the net,
What a keeper,
Dive to dive, jump to jump, save to save,
Volleys and volleys, saves to save,
The keeper comes out with the ball and shoots,
He has scored,
They have won the match by six-one,
He celebrates at each corner.

**Jonjo Hall (8)**
St Joseph's Catholic Primary School, Doncaster

## Wintertime

W intertime is finally here!
I t's time to have a snowball fight
N ow it's time for the snow to fall
T ime for hats, gloves and coats
E ach day goes by, I never want it to end
R unning around in the thick, white snow
T ime for bed, I don't mind there's another day yet
I n winter it's time for hibernation
M ost of the time you will sit at the window admiring the view
E ach snowflake has melted now springtime is here!

**Katie Harvey (10)**
St Joseph's Catholic Primary School, Doncaster

## Me And My Friends - Haiku

Me and my best friends,
Like to go to the seaside,
And eat fish and chips.

**Emerald Young (10)**
St Joseph's Catholic Primary School, Doncaster

# The White Bear

The sapphire-blue sea plunges against
The island full of snow.
As the white bear gives up his camouflage
At night.
He meanders around the wasteland of
Snow, crisp and white.
His eyes gleam of clear crystal.
His nose wet and frosty.
A mouthful of crimson blood.
His fur a pearly white.
Pawprints huge and deep.
For at night.
Under moonlight
You can see
The polar bears!

**Enya Samways (10)**
**St Joseph's Catholic Primary School, Doncaster**


# Bonfire Bonanza

Flarin' fountain
Fizzin' firecracker
Cracking cascade
Ravishing rocket
Blazin' banger
Stunning sparklers
Colourful Catherine wheels
Bonfire bonanza!

Catherine wheels all around
Bangers in the air
Finally it's Bonfire Night
*Bang! Bang!*

**Caitlin Isle (10)**
**St Joseph's Catholic Primary School, Doncaster**

# Ninjas

Ninjas, they hide around all the place,
With a grin on their face,
Doing Martial Arts
Driving in carts.

Kicking high in the air
As if it was a nightmare,
Punch rock hard
On the guard
Through they go
On the look out
For the enemy
To arrest
All the best
As if it was a quest.

Get a medal
For being a daredevil.

**Joe Dockerty (10)**
St Joseph's Catholic Primary School, Doncaster


# My Little Rocket

My little rocket flying
Right to the moon
Silver light showing
Beautiful glowing moon
On starlight night
How lovely it reminds
Me of my glowing necklace.
I love it.
Beautiful like a teardrop.

**Zoe Neocleous (10)**
St Joseph's Catholic Primary School, Doncaster

# Hurricanes

H urricanes can be very big or small
U sually they destroy everything in their path
R ampaging on and on
R uining houses and lots of land
I nstead of taking all the lives they only take a few
C ausing mass destruction
A nywhere they go
N one finds them funny
E veryone who sees them starts running
S creaming out, 'Run, run, there's a hurricane!'

**Hannelore Southern  (10)**
St Joseph's Catholic Primary School, Doncaster


# Hallowe'en

H ooray! Hooray! Hallowe'en night is here!
A mble around the streets in your costume
L ight a candle in your scary pumpkin
L augh and have lots of fun
O pen your eyes and see some freaky costumes
W alk up to doors and beg for sweets
E verybody is saying 'Trick or Treat!'
E verybody is having a great time
N obody wants Hallowe'en to end!

**Natalie McMenamin  (10)**
St Joseph's Catholic Primary School, Doncaster


# David Beckham And The Excellent Goal

Excellent striker jumpin' up and down in the air
Havin' lots of fun runnin' up and down
Dancin' around shoutin' really loud
Really happy knockin' people over
A great player.

**Aimee Vickers  (8)**
St Joseph's Catholic Primary School, Doncaster

# Christmas Eve

Christmas, Christmas what a time!
Putting tinsel up most of the night
Santa's coming with the toys
Down the chimney down he comes
Go to bed or else,
Santa won't come!
Christmas, Christmas, what a time!
Well for children anyway!
Pulling crackers and singing songs,
Playing with your toys all day long!

**Emilio Marcos Sierra (10)**
St Joseph's Catholic Primary School, Doncaster


# Whizz Whizz

Whizz whizz round and round
Under the bridge over the ridge
Oh no a crash, let's get there quick.

Number 10 racing strong going round the last corner
He's finished the race
And now he's on the podium
In first place!

**Edward Allen (11)**
St Joseph's Catholic Primary School, Doncaster


# Cool Cowboys

C harging horses riding rapidly
O ld fashioned cowboys on their saddles
W ithering deserts they ride through
B adlands full of bandits too
O n their horses they have a showdown
Y elling wildly in pain,
S uddenly silence!

**Joseph Stannard (10)**
St Joseph's Catholic Primary School, Doncaster

# Summertime

I love summertime
Oh the fresh air you breathe in!
Roses,
Love,
Pool parties, have fun!

Sweet smelling puddings,
Mum's apple pie,
Parents getting time off work,
Say goodbye to those ugly ties!

Mum and Dad have gone to the pub,
While we have sleepovers and bathe in the sun!

They don't know what we get up to,
*So go ahead;*
*Have fun!*

**Georgia Harper  (11)**
**St Joseph's Catholic Primary School, Doncaster**


# A Witch's Brew

Put the pot on, let it boil
Then throw in some cooking oil
Then throw in a fat toad's eye
Squash it up and let it fry
Then throw in some smelly pants
And right on top a cup of ants
Next put in some big fat snails
And last of all some scabby rats' tails

Want to know the name of my brew
Ask the dinner ladies
They will tell you
*It's stew!*

**Georgia Wren  (10)**
**St Joseph's Catholic Primary School, Doncaster**

## The Magic Puddle

I looked into a puddle
And guess what I could see,
Seventeen little fish
Staring back at me.

Their scales were as blue as topaz
Shining in the light
I pulled a funny face at them
It gave them quite a fright.

They pulled a face back at me
And gave a little wink,
And just to think all this time,
They could have been in my sink!

**Bronagh Gunn (11)**
**St Joseph's Catholic Primary School, Doncaster**


## We've Finished School

We've finished, we've finished
This is great!
We've got no more history and no more maths
We don't even have to go into class
Let's go to the park
Let's go to the shop
This is just like half term but forever!

I got my grades, two As and a B
I'm going to York University
Just like my uncle did
I'm going to study Astro Physics
Because I'm going to be a pilot.

**Luke Scollins (10)**
**St Joseph's Catholic Primary School, Doncaster**

# It's Christmas Eve

It is Christmas Eve
What a time, I lie in bed
Santa with his sack,
Down the chimney, down he comes
Here comes the big guy.

I can't wait for the morning,
I wonder what I'll get.
I'm getting happy, I'm feeling excited
I wonder what I'll get.

I hope I'll have an amazing day
I wonder if I'll get a bike,
I wonder if I'll get a canoe,
I wonder what I'll get.

**Daniel Johnson  (11)**
**St Joseph's Catholic Primary School, Doncaster**


# The Super Football Match

Dodgin' tacklin'

Kickin' and scorin'

Celebratin' at the same time
Our team's winnin'
Everybody's
Cheerin' and wavin'
Kickin' the ball into the goal
Everybody's shouting our team
The score is 5-1 and we're winnin'
There's only 15 minutes left
And we've won, everybody's cheerin'.

**Paige Simpson  (8)**
**St Joseph's Catholic Primary School, Doncaster**

# Going Mad

Rainin' day
What a play
Kickin' high in the sky
Havin' a splash, what a bash
Gettin' muddy, it's a goody,
The guy is mad, he is glad,
The goal is done it was fun but
Very dangerous indeed
Although he is glad he is the striker of
The year.
He's runnin' around
Off the ground
Pullin' faces and disgraces to the people around him.
Boy, he is good he's
The best bud in the world
The best striker of course.

**Grace Fielding  (8)**
**St Joseph's Catholic Primary School, Doncaster**


# Fireworks

Fireworks, fireworks
Beautiful and colourful.
Some screech, whizz and squeal
Some crackle, pop and fizzle.
They are all different shapes and sizes
From shiny sparklers to zooming rockets.
One thing I know for sure is,
All fireworks excite me.
Especially when they
          *Bang!*

**Hannah Russell  (11)**
**St Joseph's Catholic Primary School, Doncaster**

# Weather

Rain is a pain
It can spoil your games.
It smells of a dirty old drain.
But it's good for plants,
Without rain we can't live,
So rain smells of a flower train!

It's lovely when it's sunny!
It tastes like jam and honey!
But if it was always sunny,
The plants would be dry and lumpy.
So we need a bit of rain too,
But not all the time or we'd never taste jam and
Honey!

Hail makes me want to wail!
It feels like a nail,
And the cold around, bites with very sharp teeth,
Oh, I really, really hate hail!

Thunder and lightning - what a terrible storm!
It's bitterly cold out there - but in this room -
Very warm!
Thunder sounds like an elephant having a
Fight with a blue whale!
Lightning looks like fire hitting the clouds!

But after reading this poem I hope you have learnt, that
It's good for weather to be changeable,
*So don't complain next time it rains!*

**Elizabeth Martin  (8)**
**St Marie's Catholic Primary School, Sheffield**

# Beauty

Beauty is beautiful.
It smells fresh and yummy.
It tastes nice and sweet,
Like jelly in my tummy.
It feels nice like fur on mice.
It sounds wavy and crazy rolling about.
It lives in my birthday cake, every year
And when I blow my candles out everyone gives
A big cheer!

**Francesca Thomas (8)**
St Marie's Catholic Primary School, Sheffield


# Imagination

Imagination is happening in your mind
Imagination smells like a jam tart
Imagination tastes like beans
Imagination sounds like birds tweeting
Imagination feels like a trophy
Imagination lives in my mind, most of the time.

**Isaac McQuinn (8)**
St Marie's Catholic Primary School, Sheffield


# Cheerfulness

Cheerfulness, it smells like freshly baked mince pies.
Cheerfulness, it tastes like jelly and ice cream.
Cheerfulness, it sounds like popcorn popping.
Cheerfulness, it feels like a feather cushion.
Cheerfulness, it lives in Christmas.

**Daisy Shemmelds (8)**
St Marie's Catholic Primary School, Sheffield

# Love

Love is red
Love smells like roses
Love tastes like chocolate being fed to you
Love sounds like a kitten dozing in the sun
Love feels like sliding down a rainbow
Love lives everywhere.

**Rebecca Shiel  (8)**
**St Marie's Catholic Primary School, Sheffield**


# Beauty

Beauty is pink
It smells like rose perfume
It tastes like chocolate sweets from the shop
It sounds like birds singing in the treetops
It feels like soft fur from animals
It lives around the world most of the times.

**Niamh Farrell  (8)**
**St Marie's Catholic Primary School, Sheffield**


# Joy

Joy is silver
It smells like baking bread
It tastes like a super yummy chocolate bar
It sounds like my parents calling me a good girl
It feels like a super soft blanket
It lives in me.

**Georgia Oldfield  (8)**
**St Marie's Catholic Primary School, Sheffield**

# Boredom

Boredom is brown,
Boredom makes you frown
Boredom tastes like tuna chunks
Boredom smells like tuna crumbs
Boredom feels crinkly
Like an old face, wrinkly.

**Hugh Hackney  (8)**
**St Marie's Catholic Primary School, Sheffield**


# Ugliness

Ugliness is black
It smells like strawberries that are off
It tastes like rotten apples
It sounds like *yuck, yuck, yuck* all day
It feels like *big* green spots climbing up your back
It lives in the deep depths of the sea.

**JD Quinn**
**St Marie's Catholic Primary School, Sheffield**


# Joy

Joy is yellow
Joy smells like flowers
Joy tastes like fruit
Joy sounds like peace
Joy feels like fur
Joy lives in my school.

**Alice Reddin  (8)**
**St Marie's Catholic Primary School, Sheffield**

# Happiness

Happiness is like flowers growing in the garden
It is like a leaf flowing through a shiny river
Happiness is like the sun shining brightly
It tastes like ice cream with every flavour
It is like a bird flying so high it reaches Heaven
It sounds like everyone singing joyfully at church
It smells like a big juicy hot dog with ketchup
It feels like lying down in a field with soft, warm grass.

**Ian Mercado  (10)**
**St Marie's Catholic Primary School, Sheffield**


# Happiness

Happiness is flying in the air everywhere,
It smells like lime,
It tastes like watermelon,
It sounds like having fun,
It feels like your favourite thing,
It lives in the air everywhere.

**Elizabeth Briddock  (8)**
**St Marie's Catholic Primary School, Sheffield**


# Rain

Rain can go down and all around all the world.
It splitters and splatters and drops on the floor.
Splitter, splatter, splitter, splatter all around.
When will it stop? No one will know.
Splitter, splatter, splitter, splatter.
Oops all gone!

**Morgan Simpson  (8)**
**St Marie's Catholic Primary School, Sheffield**

# War

War burning down cities
People screaming
Help! Help!

Black smoke billowing from a house
Guns rattling
Bullets biting into flesh.

Blood splatting everywhere
Sulphur smelling like snake poison
People tasting it like cold metal
People being tortured
Like being stuck by mega sticky tape.

**Cameron Colclough  (8)**
St Marie's Catholic Primary School, Sheffield

# Sadness

Sadness is red.
Sadness tastes like pepper.
Sadness lives in the Devil.
Sadness smells like fire.
Sadness sounds like somebody crying.
Sadness feels like your heart is broken.

**Guido Teruzzi  (8)**
St Marie's Catholic Primary School, Sheffield

# Badness

Badness is black
It smells like rotten eggs
It tastes like sprouts
It sounds like devils stomping in Hell
It feels like a red-hot ball of red
It lives in . . . *Hell!*

**Rosey Rostant  (8)**
St Marie's Catholic Primary School, Sheffield

# Happiness

The joy of waking up to a new day
Makes me go hip hip hooray.
I climb into my mother's car
My school is not so very far.
My friends are clamouring at the gate
I'm so very glad that I'm not late.

I've had such a great start to my day
Now I'm ready to go out to play
When I've done all my work all so well
It's time for lunch, so says the bell.
With all my friends, I'll play football
The whistle goes, there's no time at all.

Once more I leave my school behind
And wait to see that dog of mine
He wags his friendly tail at me
That tail makes me feel happy see.
Once more I've had a happy day
And glad once more, upon my way.

**Dominic Casey (11)**
**St Marie's Catholic Primary School, Sheffield**


# Happiness

Happiness is red
Happiness smells like warm custard pie
Happiness tastes like melting ice cream
Happiness sounds like popcorn popping
Happiness feels like a fairy's wing
Happiness lives inside you whatever you are.

**Theresa Staub (9)**
**St Marie's Catholic Primary School, Sheffield**

# Anger

Anger sounds like the beat of a drum,
Pounding inside your head,
Anger is red like blood, glistening on a sword,
Anger looks like a red cape from a bullring,
Swirling through the air like a bird.
Anger looks like a burning building and the venom
From a snake,
Anger tastes like sour lemons, tingling on your tongue,
Anger feels like barbed wire, pressing against your
Skin, like thorns.

**Bethany Kirkbride (10)**
**St Marie's Catholic Primary School, Sheffield**


# Silence

S ilence
I s like a white
L ily carefully unfolding, floating
E venly on the water
N ever making a noise
C losing quietly in the
E vening. Still. Silent.

**Katherine Rice (10)**
**St Marie's Catholic Primary School, Sheffield**


# Hope

Hope is blue like the hottest summer's day
Hope looks like an ice sculpture at its prime
Hope smells like fresh air upon a mountain top
Hope tastes like a freshly made sandwich from Greggs
Hope feels like scoring a goal in football
Hope is great.

**Jack Clohessy (10)**
**St Marie's Catholic Primary School, Sheffield**

# Anger

I was on my way to school one day
I stopped at the swings and decided to play
The bell just rang, I tried to jump off
But I got in a tangle and landed with a flop.

Am I happy, or am I sad?
For as all I know, it is that bad
When I eyed this person, with all my hope
I asked, 'Can you help me?' but she said 'Nope!'

So there I am feeling down in the dumps
My knee hurting badly, I've got bruises and bumps
I hear the girl sniggering, is she sniggering at me?
The bell for break went, how bad can this be?

I guess I should get up, but then something caught my eye
It's Miss Strotely, my teacher, 'Oh my, oh my!'
I hope I'm not in trouble, what did I, do wrong?
But then she picks me up, wow! She's strong!

I can't tell on the girl for not helping me, I'm not a snitch
I spoke to soon, because out comes Mr Flitch
Beside him the girl, whose name I do not know
I couldn't help myself, I shouted 'I told you so!'

Miss, this girl, she's really mean
All she does all day is eat jelly beans
Yet she can't be bothered to help me up
But who does she treat better? Mr Snuffles her pup.

I start to run off, run away
Hopefully, I'll be gone by the end of the day
Mr Flitch catches up with me, hasn't he had enough?
And this goes to show, that life is rough
. . . 'Did you get that?'

**Ifeoma Ezepue  (10)**
**St Marie's Catholic Primary School, Sheffield**

# Make Me Happy

Oh dear, oh dear,
What can I say?
I'm feeling very ill today.

Yesterday was cheery,
Now it seems oh so dreary.

Oh dear, oh dear,
What can I do?
I think I must have caught the flu.

Here I lie, very still,
I wish I wasn't oh so ill.

My head is burning,
My tummy churning.

I call the doctor
'Come with haste
And put a smile back on my face.'

**Katie Farrell  (11)**
**St Marie's Catholic Primary School, Sheffield**

# The Seasons

December, January, February
Is very, very snowy, though watch for the buds
Of the new summer berries.

March, April, May
Can be a little little rainy but when it's sunny
You might want to go and play.

June comes soon
July flies by
August, September you might want to
Remember.

October, November
Cold, cold, cold, so keep warm by the fire's embers.

**Niamh Grant  (8)**
**St Marie's Catholic Primary School, Sheffield**

# Dizzy

Dizzy is blurred
And spread out
It's messy and
Mixed up too
But it sounds like
People, crowds
Of people
It's complicated
But simple
It's easy but hard
Dizzy tastes like
Spaghetti all coiling
In my mouth
It smells like popcorn
Sweet but sour
Dream catchers, bright
Colours, they all
Remind me of
Dizzy too
Dizzy is free, trapped
Loud but quiet
Dizzy is an everlasting
Gasp for air
The colours of dizzy are
Pink and flowery,
Just like in fun fairs,
That reminds me of dizzy too!

**Agatha Milner  (10)**
**St Marie's Catholic Primary School, Sheffield**

# Sadness

I feel sad and gloomy when there's coldness in the air.
The wind is blowing madly
And there are snowflakes in my hair.
I feel sad and gloomy when people laugh and stare.
I have no friends at all,
And no one really cares.
I feel sad and gloomy when my mum tells me off,
When my sister plays mean tricks on me,
And my brother starts to cough,
And as I'm lying on my bed,
The nightmares come and go
About the things that have happened to me
About my friends and foes.

**Martha Scattergood & Eleri Kirkpatrick-Lorente  (9)**
St Marie's Catholic Primary School, Sheffield


# Mischief

Mischief is red
It smells like tomato sauce
It tastes like cream cake
It sounds like titter, titter, laugh, laugh
It feels like a climbing frame
It jumps up in my mind.

**Ryan Tweddell  (8)**
St Marie's Catholic Primary School, Sheffield


# Frightened

Frightened is a dark deep blue,
Dangling around my heart,
Frightened is a cold empty space
Filled with love and a heart,
Fright.

**Reece Major  (8)**
St Theresa's Catholic Primary School, Sheffield

# Friends!

F is for friendship forever and always
R is for responsible in many different ways
I is for incredible we will never fall apart
E is for everlasting whatever maybe
N is for nice as calm as the sea
D is for daylight it will never go away
S is for sunshine that will always be beside us

*That's what makes our friendship the best!*

**Hannah O'Rourke & Alicia Farrell  (10)**
St Theresa's Catholic Primary School, Sheffield


# Daydreamy

Daydreamy is all around you in your head.
Daydreamy is a really light colour, it is white.
Daydreamy is a big circle in your head.
It is filled with happiness bubbling inside you,
It makes me feel lots of adventurous things.
I have a different day dream every day.
Daydreamy makes me feel happy and funny.
Daydreamy is a very nice thing in me, it is great.

**Megan Torpey  (8)**
St Theresa's Catholic Primary School, Sheffield


# Joyful

Joyful is a light blue,
Getting you happy when you are down.
It is in your smile, and it makes sure you don't frown.
It is a hexagon, making sure you're always alright.
It is full of excitement and laughter
Joyful makes me happy and makes me laugh.

**Kieran Beer  (9)**
St Theresa's Catholic Primary School, Sheffield

# Powerful Potion

Ear of pig, tail of rat,
Eye of sheep, wing of bat.
Tongue of owl, slime of snake
Lips of dog that I love to bake.

*Children and adults count to nine,*
*Then I will have done the potion of mine . . .*

Octopus leg, toenail of a tiger
Added with a big, juicy spider.
Shell of turtle, tail of a cat
Stir it up wow look at that!

*Children and adults count to nine,*
*Then I will have done the potion of mine . . .*

**Chloe Timms (11)**
**St Theresa's Catholic Primary School, Sheffield**


# Terrified

Terrified is a deep dark brown
Dangling around inside me
Terrified is a cold square
Filled with fear
Terrified is a feeling of
Scariness and tears.

**Courtney Wright (8)**
**St Theresa's Catholic Primary School, Sheffield**


# Annoyed

Annoyed is a ruby-red
You can find it in your brain,
Annoyed is a circle,
It makes me think of irritating things.

**Ellie-Marie Ottewell (8)**
**St Theresa's Catholic Primary School, Sheffield**

# Mix The Magic

Ear of elephant, nose of dog,
Nail of mouldy hedgehog
Beads of bracelet, pus from spot,
Put it into my boiling pot.

Cauldron, cauldron do your trouble,
And mix the magic spell!

Ear from rabbit, tail from cat,
Eye from hippo, fur from rat
Teeth from shark, eye of girl
In the sea lay a beautiful pearl.

Cauldron, cauldron, do your trouble
And mix the magic spell!

Ear of rabbit, slimy toe of frog,
Mouldy persons bowl of sprog
Lead pencil, hairy ear of dog
Sweat of man after his jog.

Cauldron, cauldron, do your trouble
And mix the magic spell!

**Annie Wood (10)**
St Theresa's Catholic Primary School, Sheffield


# Excited

Excited is a light pale pink,
In your heart drifting like a balloon,
Excited is a big massive circle,
Filled with a calm and peaceful emotion
With love floating all around it,
It makes me feel happy but calm
Inside.

**Hana Riaz (9)**
St Theresa's Catholic Primary School, Sheffield

# Putrid Pot

Vicious venom from a snake,
And malodorous seaweed found from a lake.
Eye of newt and head of dog,
Which has been liking from a dank, dark bog.

Put all in the putrid pot
Until it becomes so very, hot!

Foot of an elephant, bones of dog,
Put these pieces of skin in the pot
Spiders with venom, slug slime,
Put them in this pot of mine.

Put all in the putrid pot
Until it becomes so very, hot!

A mouldy tooth of cat,
Put a toad which looks really fat,
A pupil from an old dumbstruck dog,
This spell is starting to get hot.

Put all in the putrid pot,
Until it becomes so very hot.

**John Zurita  (11)**
**St Theresa's Catholic Primary School, Sheffield**


# Sad

Sad is a dark deep blue
It's when I lost my toys
The shape is square
It's filled with tears
It makes me sad.

**Tyler Brown  (8)**
**St Theresa's Catholic Primary School, Sheffield**

# Mixture From Madness

Ear of an elephant bones of a dog,
Put these pieces of skin in the pot.
Snakes with venom, snail slime,
Put them in this pot of mine.

Double, double, toil and trouble
Fire burn and cauldron bubble.

Old mouldy teeth of a bat,
Put a frog which looks really fat.
An eye from an old mouldy dog,
This spell is starting to get hot.

Double, double, toil and trouble,
Fire burn and cauldron bubble.

**Tumi Gopalang (10)**
**St Theresa's Catholic Primary School, Sheffield**


# Cooking Time Twist

Ear of a weasel, leg of a dog,
Eye of a mouldy rotten owl.
An ear of a sweaty eagle,
Put this in the pot of mine.

Cauldron, cauldron, make this spell
Cooking all terribly well.

Wings of 100 angels, a tail of a cat.
A wing of a crow, poo of a cow.
Nose of a frog, snakes' slime.
Put them in this pot of mine.

**Jordan Barnes (10)**
**St Theresa's Catholic Primary School, Sheffield**

# Here Comes Trouble

Eye of chicken,
You'll be lickin'
Blood of blind bat,
If it do plant will scat.

Double trouble make me a rotten bubble,
Don't come or there is trouble!

Rabies of rat,
Two stupid bats
Slime of slugs
More of bugs.

Double trouble make a rotten bubble,
Don't come or there is trouble!

Death of owl,
Hounds will howl
Storm of lightning
Athena will be fighting.

Double trouble make a rotten bubble,
Don't come or there is trouble!

**Kaine Wild (10)**
**St Theresa's Catholic Primary School, Sheffield**

# Trouble And Strife

Tooth of a dog, tail of a rabbit,
Rotten through with spear will stab it.
Scale of a fish and fin of a whale,
Wind of storm, lightning and hail.

Here we go, let's boil and bubble,
Cauldron's making lots of trouble.

**Joe McNally (10)**
**St Theresa's Catholic Primary School, Sheffield**

# Gruesome Gruel

Tail of a rat, head of hog,
Tongue of a disgusting daunting dog.
Plop goes the head of one plump pig
And the two pairs of legs of a guinea pig!

Mix it, mix it till it's nice and green,
Aren't I really very mean . . .

Nose of a monkey, paw of a cat,
Smell of a horrible bat, bat, bat.
Muck of an old crumbled sock,
And the noise of a clock that goes click clock.

Mix it, mix it till it's nice and green,
Aren't I really very mean . . .

**Kiera Burgin (11)**
**St Theresa's Catholic Primary School, Sheffield**


# Mixture Madness

Ear of elephant as big as a log,
Along came the three witches
And turned it into a dog.

Eye of cat, toe of a dog,
Mix it up and make some fog.

Bubble, bubble, trouble make
Put it in the oven to bake.

Hair of horse, noise of pig,
And then turn it into a blonde wig.

**Hannah Miles (10)**
**St Theresa's Catholic Primary School, Sheffield**

# Cauldron Chaos

Ear of rat, head of frog,
Eyeball of a mouldy snake.
Big pig's head and slimy old sock,
Put them in the pot and never ever stop.

Bubble bubble mix and double
Toad's eye boil and cauldron bubble.

Tail of cat, eye of rat,
Mouth of bat, teeth of cat,
Tail of dog, fin of fish,
Mix, mix, stir it well
To make a potion for a spell.

Bubble bubble mix it well
To make a deadly cauldron.

Wood of log, tooth of shark,
Then take a bit of a puppy's bark.
Mix it well to be the best,
Let's make sure not to make a mess.

**Erica Bothamley (10)**
**St Theresa's Catholic Primary School, Sheffield**


# Sad

Sad is a dark, dark blue,
Hanging in the woods,
Sad is a big ball,
Filled with worrying water,
Sad is an empty ball
Like worrying water,
It is scary and lonely,
Sad is the most saddest.

**Imogen Norcliffe (8)**
**St Theresa's Catholic Primary School, Sheffield**

# Year 6

There I stood in Year 6 -
Just about to pick some sticks . . .
Just about to write a bunch -
Straight away I had my lunch!

There we stood on the pitch -
Just about to fall in a ditch . . .
The ball was kicked up in the sky!
My, oh my I don't know why?

There we went back into class,
A minute later a piece of glass
Smashed,
After that it was time for dance,
After that we learnt about romance!

**Jordan Scarborough (11)**
**St Theresa's Catholic Primary School, Sheffield**


# Drop Them In!

Tail of a lizard, eye of dragon,
A rotten rat pulled out of a wagon.
Tongue of a mouldy stinkin' toad,
A few rotten squirrels scraped off the road,

Everyone here count to five
Then drop in a mouldy hive!

Tail of a jaw-ripping huge T-rex,
Ten ants' droppings that are micro specs.
Claw of a puma, tail of a tiger,
Two more pints of rotten cider.

Everyone here count to five,
Then drop in a mouldy hive!

**Harry Atkinson (10)**
**St Theresa's Catholic Primary School, Sheffield**

# Special Spell

Sinister slithering snakes of slime,
Put them in this pot of mine,
Ear of elephant, head of dog,
Then put in a rotten frog.

Bubble, bubble, bubble pop,
Making spells I'll never stop!

Ear of cat, tail of rat,
Mouth of dog, and wing of bat.
Poo of panda, eye of toad,
And a brick of mucky road.

Bubble, bubble, bubble, pop,
Making spells I'll never stop!

**Hannah O'Rourke (10)**
**St Theresa's Catholic Primary School, Sheffield**

# Spellbound

Bones of elephant, tail of rat,
Hairballs of the fat juicy cat.
Sinister slithering snake in trouble,
Then the cauldron will begin to bubble.

One, two, three, four here
We go,
Let the cauldron overflow.

Teeth of shark, legs of dog,
Chopped up small upon a log,
Beak of birds, wings from duck,
The spell is done and you're in bad luck!

**Mollie Wood (10)**
**St Theresa's Catholic Primary School, Sheffield**

# Trouble Bubble

Snails and slugs and ugly bugs' buds.
A chimpanzee running from a bumblebee.
Now it's double trouble
Let the cauldron do its trouble!

Frog's eye as it goes by,
Anteater's tongue as it goes along
Now it's double trouble
Let the cauldron do it's trouble.

Poo of a baby snake
Guts out of a koala.
So we can bake, bake, bake,
Now it's double trouble
Let the cauldron do its trouble!

**Jordan Loftus  (11)**
**St Theresa's Catholic Primary School, Sheffield**


# Untitled

Upset is a dark, deep blue
It hangs around your heart like a heavy load
Upset is a big sad face in your heart
It's filled with watery tears.
Upset is when you have lost something
If you have lost somebody who has died
It makes you think of upsetting things
It makes your heart beat very fast
It is dreadful when something happens upsetting
Upset is a feeling of lost
A lonely, worrying, empty emotion.

**Sharna Burgin  (8)**
**St Theresa's Catholic Primary School, Sheffield**

# Boil, Boil, Bake, Bake

A tail of a donkey, leg of a rat
Come on along and I'll throw in a bat
Slithering snails and sucking slugs
Then we'll drop in a couple of bugs.

Boil, boil, bake, bake
There we go, it's a piece of cake.

The eye of dragon, as big as a car
You can see the eye from far, far, far
Drop in a drop of slime
Keep on going there is no time.

Boil, boil, bake, bake
There we go, it's a piece of cake.

The lips of a horse, the stomach of a pig
Come on let's throw in a wig
An octopus' leg, tooth of a shark,
Don't be scared, it's only the dark.

Boil, boil, bake, bake
There we go, it's a piece of cake.

**Danielle Platton (10)**
**St Theresa's Catholic Primary School, Sheffield**


# Angry Ashley!

Angry is a colour of brown,
It is a frightening dream
It is a circle of brown
Filled with hatred and
Terrifying words.

The word angry
Is an unthoughtful word
Your heart beats fast
When you are angry.

**Ashley Lane (8)**
**St Theresa's Catholic Primary School, Sheffield**

# Worried

Worried is a dark dull colour
Hanging around yourself as a
Huge black blob,
Worried is a dull star,
It's filled with worry in your heart,
It makes you feel lonely and worried,
Feels like I am on my own
Forever and ever.

**Libia Mae Stachiw (8)**
**St Theresa's Catholic Primary School, Sheffield**

# Scared

Scared is a shimmer of black,
And a swirling circle of darkness,
It is in the darkest dream,
Scared is filled with fear and horrible thoughts.

Screams, it makes me think of black dark nightmares
They are a smirk of fear and are heartless.

**Charlotte Colk (9)**
**St Theresa's Catholic Primary School, Sheffield**

# Mad

Mad is the colour dark red
Mad is all around us
Mad is a circle
Mad makes me feel like
Hurting someone mad.

**Nathan Mason (9)**
**St Theresa's Catholic Primary School, Sheffield**

# Tired

Tired is a dark
Deep blue
Dangling from
Your heart like a
Real heavy load.
Tired is a small square,
Filled in your heart.

**Shelby-Jo Chambers  (8)**
St Theresa's Catholic Primary School, Sheffield

# Strawberries

Strawberries are yummy,
feels good when they enter your tummy.

Strawberries are juicy,
they are fruity.

Strawberries are sweet,
like a tangy treat.

Strawberries are soft and red,
truly scrumptious . . .

**Corie Wagstaffe  (10)**
Shafton Primary School

# My Pets

Bubble is grey
And Squeak is black
They are my pet rabbits
And I love them to bits

My brother John is like Humpty Dumpty
Because he sits on walls
And tumbles and falls.

**Chloe Lindley  (7)**
Shafton Primary School

# My Favourite Fruit

It is a big circle and on the top it has a green stalk
But when I open the window all I smell is pork
It has a smooth-looking skin
But when I feel it, it goes in the bin.

It looks rough in some places and smooth in others
I certainly don't share it with my brothers
They smell sour and sometimes sweet
I always eat them sat on a seat.

When you rip off the skin it sounds really weird
I certainly won't give it to a man with a beard
When you bite it, it makes a little crunch
I love it when they come in a bunch.

When it is sour it is tangy but when it's sweet it is delicious
I definitely know it's nutritious.

Can you guess what my favourite fruit is?

**Holly Lockwood  (10)**
**Shafton Primary School**

# The Little Boy And Girl

The little boy and girl forgot to clean out the cage,
A rabbit must be lucky to have an owner like you Paige.
The rabbit knocked over the fish
And then it's thirsty again.
Some people do not notice he's in pain,
It's smelly and dirty
And he's very sick.
He needs to go to the vets.
The little boy and girl
Wish they had him now,
Forever he's in Heaven.

**Bethany Cawston  (9)**
**Shafton Primary School**

# Little Fish Captivity

Little fish, little fish caged into the smallest dish
Swimming round and round all day
Then ask my friends to come and play.

They point and prod and stare at him
One of them put their hand in
And nearly ripped off his fin.

Little fish, little fish why are you inside that little dish?
You should be free in the river or the sea
Look at the top of the water a bee is after me.

**Connor Cocks (8)**
**Shafton Primary School**


# My Mountain View

I was a gigantic mountain just below the baking hot sun
I was never ever freezing
Of course I was only a few metres below a gigantic sphere of fire.

My mountain view never ever stopped
It went on and on and on forever.

I could see the world turning around me
I could see forests, homes, cars, rivers and so on.

The people on the ground looked like tiny spots
I could feel the gentle breeze blowing around me.

**Daniel Sykes (7)**
**Shafton Primary School**

# Grapes

The watery juice runs down my chin
When I am chewing them.

Grapes are delicious just like my wishes.

Lovely grapes they make my day.

I eat my grapes in a phone booth
As they are so very, very smooth.

I think grapes are crunchy
When they are in their bunches.

**Alex Goddard  (11)**
Shafton Primary School


# The Fluffy Ginger Fox

Fluffy, ginger and brown
Running through the town

Around the farm, chickens he chased
In-between the pigs and cows he raced

Vegetables are not for him
Just look at the fox's cheeky grin

At last he found a juicy goat
Watch out or he'll have you by the throat.

**Jake Arrowsmith  (8)**
Shafton Primary School


# My Favourite Food

My favourite food is rosy red
Smooth and fragrant it can be said
Glossy, juicy, delicious too
I can recommend this apple to you.

**Lewisham Screaton  (10)**
Shafton Primary School

# Strawberry

Heart-shaped with dips in the skin
Quite small and bumpy
Inside the skin its colour's light pink
Luscious also succulent
It's got a soothing taste
Tantalising
Tangy
It's my favourite fruit
It would be a shame to let it waste.

**Elizabeth Wignall  (10)**
Shafton Primary School


# Apple

Red, round, rosy apples
Crispy, crunching and chewy
Tastes juicy and sweet
Tastes so good to me.

Thick, furry, rough skin
The juice runs down your chin
The skin is shiny and reflective
Tastes fantastic to me.

**Ryan Hewitt  (11)**
Shafton Primary School


# Mashed Potatoes And Gravy

Mashed potatoes and gravy
Feels soft
Like a fluffy cloud floating in the sky
Covered in thick, runny, beefy gravy
*Ahh! Bisto*
Tastes creamy and buttery
Mouth-watering.

**Kyle Cooper  (10)**
Shafton Primary School

# Popcorn Poem

Before the popcorn's popped
You could say it's minute
So dense, so smooth and lustrous,
Beautifully golden, not silver like a flute.

The space it takes is smaller
When it is still corn
Sounds and feels tickly
Takes more space as popcorn.

It's exciting to wait for the popping
The volcano erupting sound
Exploding, crackling, banging
The noise doesn't cost a pound.

Feels like fluffy cotton wool
Fresh, picked off the bush
It doesn't taste of very much
Bite into it, *crunch! crunch!*

**Becky Hirst  (10)**
**Shafton Primary School**


# My Favourite Food

My favourite food looks shiny and glossy
But don't share it with me, I'll turn bossy
It feels as smooth as a baby's bottom
But sometimes really rotten
Smells as good as a rose
When you eat it you've just got to pose
It tastes really crunchy
But really munchy
It's an apple.

**Alice Whittaker  (10)**
**Shafton Primary School**

# Why, Why Is The Rabbit In Prison?

Why, why, why am I in prison?
I like to see the full moon
Why? Why? I want freedom
I wish it was June.

Why, why am I in prison?
This cage is never clean
Why? Why? I want freedom
I want this cage to gleam.

Why, why am I in prison?
I want to play
Why? Why? I want freedom
And it's my favourite day.

Why, why am I in prison?
I go really dark black
Why? Why? I want freedom
They take me back in a sack

**Jack Sephton (8)**
Shafton Primary School

# Pigs In Blankets

I put them on a tray
and hope and pray.

They go with Christmas dinner
but they're gone in a spinner.

They give the kitchen a smokey smell
but then comes Auntie Dell.

They look gorgeous on my plate
but they don't know their own fate.

**Thomas Birkin (10)**
Shafton Primary School

# A Knight And A Queen

A knight and a queen
lived in a limousine
The queen was so mean
she didn't want to be seen.

The knight was so bad
he didn't have a dad
His dad was so mad
he was a tiny bit bad.

Her mum was so good
she needed Robin Hood
The knight zoomed off
leaving his cloth
The Queen was bad
but she wanted her dad.

**Harry Francis  (7)**
**Shafton Primary School**


# Red Delight

A sweet and sour heart
Rough on the outside
Smooth on the inside
Smells juicy
Fresh
Ready to eat
Tastes fragrant, bitter
Mouth-watering and yummy
Pliable inside
Squidgy
Silent pleasure.

**Lewis Briggs  (10)**
**Shafton Primary School**

# Tropical Dream

Pineapples have lumpy brown skin
I always put it in the bin
Juice drips down my slippery chin
When I bite in

Juicy yellow flesh
It is the best
I make sure it doesn't
Go down my vest.

**Megan Hamer  (11)**
**Shafton Primary School**


# Crocodile

If I was a crocodile
I'd grind my teeth
and snap my mouth
I'd be a big food thief
I'd be fast, not slow
I'd like cold
and could grow very old
*I'm watching you*
*Boo! I'm going to catch you.*

**Myles Goddard  (8)**
**Shafton Primary School**


# Apple

Rosy red apples
Bright as can be
Shining in the sun
Spherical and juicy
Firm and healthy
Crunch! Crunch! Crunch!

**Jacob Millard  (10)**
**Shafton Primary School**

# My Favourite Fruit

My favourite fruit is really sweet
As I give myself a treat.

It smells as fragrant as a flower
As it gives me lots of power.

Mostly red and green
Watch out, they turn me mean.

Can you guess what I like?
It's small and round, like Uncle Mike!

**Kristie Shelton (10)**
Shafton Primary School


# My Dog

I can't understand why I'm here all alone,
I hate to moan
Why, oh why do I have to stay here?
But I have to do tricks for my trainer Mia.
I have performed in shows of all kinds of weather, rain or shine,
It is not fine.
I have to go on a lead when I should run free,
They do not care for me.

**Georgie-Lee Chapman (9)**
Shafton Primary School


# The Tanked Snake

The snake should not be in a tank,
His name's not Fred, nor Frank.
He should be in the jungle slithering in the night,
But now he's got just a red light.
The snake has to go very, very soon,
Or he'll die in pain, beyond the moon.

**Lewis Horsbrough (8)**
Shafton Primary School

# If I Were A Butterfly

If I were a butterfly I'd keep on flying around.
If I were a butterfly I'd fly on pollen every day.
If I were a butterfly I'd lie in the sun all alone.
If I were a butterfly I'd fly in the clouds happy.
If I were a butterfly I'd be very spotty and very pink and orange
And so would my friends.
I would be very strong.
I'd try to sing.
If I were a butterfly I'd be very stingy.
If I were a butterfly I'd keep on winning.

**Sasha Haynes (8)**
Shafton Primary School

# A Fish In Captivity

A fish in a bowl all alone
dreaming of being back home

A fish bowl is so small
please can someone take down the glass wall

A wall so strong
so can I sing a song?

Can I have a new home?
The dog has a bone when I am groaning.

Please help me!

**Jordan Hinchliffe (8)**
Shafton Primary School

# Snake

I went to a zoo to see a snake
I knocked on the glass, he was awake
A slippery snake was on the floor
I went to pick it up but he went to bite me more.

**Kieren Saxton (8)**
Shafton Primary School

## Monday's Child

Monday's child is good at football,
Tuesday's child is very small.
Wednesday's child is loud and barmy,
Thursday's child joined the Army.
Friday's child has twisty knickers,
Saturday's child eats all the Snickers.
The child that is born on the Sabbath Day
is bone idle and sleeps his life away.

**Kenny Sweeney (7)**
**Waverley Primary School**


## Monday's Child

Monday's child climbed up the tree,
Tuesday's child won't eat her tea.
Wednesday's child plays with her toys,
Thursday's child makes lots of noise.
Friday's child is very nosy,
Saturday's child has a posy.
The child that's born on the Sabbath Day
Is full of love in every way.

**Eyea Ballah (7)**
**Waverley Primary School**


## Monday's Child

Monday's child is very hairy,
Tuesday's child is a good fairy.
Wednesday's child can be rude,
Thursday's child likes his food.
Friday's child is nice and cosy,
Saturday's child is very nosy.
The child that's born on the Sabbath Day
visits to play.

**Ian Rathbone (7)**
**Waverley Primary School**

## Monday's Child

Monday's child has a fat belly,
Tuesday's child eats lots of jelly.
Wednesday's child has a fast car,
Thursday's child is at the bar.
Friday's child has a long-haired dolly,
Saturday's child has an orange lolly.
And the child that is born on the Sabbath Day
is the one that will pay the banker today.

**Nicole Spencer  (8)**
Waverley Primary School


## Monday's Child

Monday's child is loud and noisy
Tuesday's child is warm and cosy
Wednesday's child is really nosy
Thursday's child has been so dozy
Friday's child is very homely
Saturday's child looks oh so rosy
The child that is born on the Sabbath Day
Is oh so happy.

**Ashley Law  (7)**
Waverley Primary School


## Monday's Child

Monday's child is a hippy,
Tuesday's child is very dippy.
Wednesday's child is big and fat,
Thursday's child has a woolly hat.
Friday's child is extremely mad,
Saturday's child is always sad.
The child that is born on the Sabbath Day
is lazy and mardy but I love him, OK?

**Alex Jenkinson  (7)**
Waverley Primary School

# The Forbidden Corner

The forbidden corner
What do I see?
I see a red devil
And dangling ghosts
The forbidden corner
That's what I see.

The forbidden corner
What do I hear?
Massive burping noises
The birds tweeting
The forbidden corner
That's what I hear.

The forbidden corner
What do I feel?
I feel scared with the goosebumps
I am happy in
The forbidden corner
That's what I feel.

The forbidden corner
What do I like?
I like finding clues
I like the red devil pool
The forbidden corner
That's what I like.

**Shona Brown  (7)**
**Waverley Primary School**

# The Forbidden Corner

The forbidden corner
What do I see?
I see the big tree
With the grumpy face
The forbidden corner
That's what I see.

The forbidden corner
What do I hear?
I hear fear
From the talking walls
The forbidden corner
That's what I hear.

The forbidden corner
What do I feel?
I feel water dripping on me
And it's getting me wet
The forbidden corner
That's what I feel.

The forbidden corner
What do I like?
I like the burping castle
With the funny tonsil
The forbidden corner
That's what I like.

**Olivia Hartle  (7)**
**Waverley Primary School**

## Teddy Bear

I am a teddy
I have one eye
and a stitch on my ear
But the little girl cuddles me
even if I have one eye
and a stitch on my ear
I live on her cushion all day long
But her big brother hurts me
by throwing me on the ground
that makes me cry.

**Chloe Hawcroft  (8)**
**Waverley Primary School**


## What Am I?

I am slimy and slow.
Not many girls like me
I eat boring grass
You cannot see me
I come out in the rain
I have patterns on me
You cannot quite see them
I hide in the soil
I drink water a lot.

**Tia Katey Gleadall  (7)**
**Waverley Primary School**


## What Am I?

I am a book,
People like reading me,
I am orange and my pictures are good.
My story is interesting.
It tells you about the three bears
And the broken stool or hot porridge bowl.

**Nathan Morgan  (8)**
**Waverley Primary School**

# What Am I?

My name is Chloe,
I wear a blue glittery dress,
I wear white gloves,
I ride in a truck with pictures of me,
I love it when you play with me,
I come with a white coat,
You can take my shoes off,
I have high-heeled shoes on my feet,
I loved the day you took me out of the box,
You love me.

**Rayanne Basley-Cox  (7)**
Waverley Primary School

# Monday's Child

Monday's child will use a pen,
Tuesday's child has a pet hen.
Wednesday's child has a snail,
Thursday's child paints her nails.
Friday's child plays in a puddle,
Saturday's child gets in a muddle.
The child that is born on the Sabbath Day
asked her mum to go out to play.

**Natasha Morgan  (8)**
Waverley Primary School

# Sun And Rain

R aindrops splashing on the ground
A nd dripping on the rooftops
I n the garden you are getting wet
N ear the fence rushing down

S hine brightly in your eyes
U sually behind the cloud
N ormally cold.

**Javian Abiad  (9)**
Willow Primary School

# My Weather Feelings

When it is raining
I feel cold and wet,
When the wind breezes
It is so calm and dull.

When it is sunny
I feel hot and happy,
When I swim in the pool
I feel cool and excited.

When it is snowing
It is so cold and soft,
When I go to sleep
I feel warm and cosy.

When leaves are falling
I crunch and collect,
When I look at leaves
I feel warm because of all the colours.

**Laura McKirdy  (9)**
**Willow Primary School**

# Weapons

The swords stab through
bloodthirsty victims
with pride and power.
Bow and arrow
flying through the air
eventually hitting its target,
Canons fired with amazement
in feared human eyes.
Spear, long but thin weapon
with its deadly point.

**William Feborov  (8)**
**Willow Primary School**

# Christmas

Christmas time
Is best of all
When we go out
And make snowballs.

Even the twins
Behave themselves
Thinking they might see
Santa and his elves.

Together we eat
Drink and play
It's such a pleasant
And happy day.

When Christmas is over
I feel so sad
But thinking of Easter
Makes me glad.

**Lakhpreet Kaur (8)**
**Willow Primary School**

# Willow School

W illow School rocks,
 I n school we work hard,
 L earning every day,
 L oving each other,
 O n time every week,
W illow School, uniforms looking smart.

 S chool playgrounds softening,
 C ool headbands, hair ties and shoes,
 H ead teacher telling teachers what to do,
 O livia get to work,
 O scar sit down,
 L earn right now!

**Liana Haynes (8)**
**Willow Primary School**

# Feelings

Beautiful clouds wandering around,
It crashes my feelings full with sadness . . .
I am now alone, sitting here,
Feeling so blind, glimpse of dullness.
Such a cruel world, no happiness, no sound,
White droplets of tears running down my cheek.
It's so empty, evil and cold . . .
Now here I am, it's an empty world.
A light gleams upon my face,
The dullness is gone.
He asks what my name is.
I don't respond.
Just a smile upon my gleaming face.
Someone is here . . . a true friend forever.

So there is happiness in the *world*.

**Sidney Choi  (9)**
**Willow Primary School**

# Cats And Dogs

Cats are very clean animals,
they use their tongues to clean themselves.
Cats can be a variety of colours,
most cats like being tickled on their tummies and stroked.
Lots of people like cats, they are furry and cuddly
but you always lose them.

Dogs are mostly clean but you have to wash them
but dogs are very nice animals.
Dogs can have a variety of colours,
they love being walked and stroked.
They like playing games and catching cats.

**Phoebe Ramsbottom  (8)**
**Willow Primary School**

# Magic Box

*(Based on 'Magic Box' by Kit Wright)*

I will put in my box . . .
The gleam of the morning sun,
The scent of the morning wind,
The wind, the moon and the sun.

I will put in my box . . .
The sparkling puddles on the ground,
The raindrops dripping on the rooftops,
The thunderstorm in my mind.

I will put in my box . . .
The even mind of my afternoon sun
And the potato growing in the watering mud,
My feeling of the midnight moon.

I will put in my box . . .
The morning sound that is still in my mind,
The red morning sun burning my eyes,
The sound of owls in the midnight moon.

I will put in my box . . .
The midnight smell of warm bacon,
Not to forget about my morning breakfast,
The cold breeze at 10pm.

I will put in my box . . .
The brightest picture in my feelings,
The feeling I have ever made,
The brightest sunlight I have ever seen.

I will think about my box,
Put my best feelings in my box,
Send my feelings near and far,
Give my fears away.

**Shane Salmon  (9)**
**Willow Primary School**

# I Feel Like A Raindrop

I feel like a raindrop, crying as I fall,
So little, so small that no one cares at all.

As I hit the ground with lots of cries,
I know some people are sad inside.

People jump and stamp in the little puddles,
But when you do you put us raindrops in a muddle.

We can't find family, we can't find friends,
I feel like it will never end.

But I hope in a day or two I'll feel happy and so will you,
Even if it takes a year, a day or a night, I will be happy
some time soon!

**Hannah Skipp (9)**
**Willow Primary School**


# Raindrops

Raindrops spitting like a snake
Raindrops dripping on the rooftops

Rain
drop
dropping
on the
ground
making
puddles
waiting to
be found
Splash!
Splash!

**Paige Durdy (9)**
**Willow Primary School**

# Raindrops

I got out of bed, it felt
like it was Doomsday. I
thought it was spitting water
like a python. I got into the car, it
was like a shelter for World War II.
I thought it was blistery winds. In the
playground somebody came up to me,
he was nice.

**Elliott Tong  (9)**
Willow Primary School

# What I Can See

I can see the big green oak tree
I can see the gleaming lamp post shining on me
I can see the wind blowing the leaves
I can see some more big green oak trees
I can see the small black dirty drain
I can see the small drips of rain
I can see the big conkers fall to the ground
Smooth and round.

**Lauren Playfoot  (8)**
Willow Primary School

# Why?

Why do we have to eat tea?
Why do kids usually play with toys?
Why do bees collect pollen?
Why do we sing hymns in church?
Why do we count from one to infinity?
Why?
Why?
Why?

**Maxwell Abbott  (8)**
Willow Primary School

# Sir Autumn

Sir Autumn has come,
with his army of wind,
chasing summer away,
Sir Autumn is here.

Sir Autumn has come,
squeezing conkers from their spiky flesh,
ripping leaves from skeleton trees
and slicing the corn with his icy sabre.

Sir Autumn has come,
days darken as his army spreads
and scatters through the land,
while he battles for eternal darkness.

Sir Autumn is defeated,
he is sure he will return,
now his reign has ended,
Lady Winter has just begun.

**Adam Wilson & Danial Mohammed  (10)**
**Willow Primary School**


# Raindrops Clear

R eception is hard,
A t the age of 4,
I  was crying because I wanted my mum,
N athan, my friend, wasn't my friend,
D ifferent teacher, different routine,
R ory my cuddly toy disappeared,
O ops my teacher shouted at me,
P roper hard work,
S ad, dull, cold and lonely.

C oming my way,
L ittle did I know,
E lliott my mate from footie,
A ny badness no!
R eally happy to go free and run!

**Millie Gilkes  (9)**
**Willow Primary School**

# Autumn

Autumn has arrived!
Frightened the sun far away,
Stripping the trees bare,
As animals hide away.

Autumn has arrived!
Conkers jump out of their shells,
Leaves rustle in a bitter wind,
As she turns cobwebs into jewellery.

Autumn has arrived!
Dark evenings spread over the Earth,
Children go trick or treating,
Bonfires gradually die down.

Autumn has arrived!
She flies through the mist,
Destroying anything in her way,
Trees and leaves prepare to fight.

**Josh Horgan & James Sneddon  (10)**
**Willow Primary School**


# Animals

The dolphin glides
The monkey chirps
The snake slithers and cats crawl
Animals are beautiful, animals are wonderful
They make you feel happy when you are feeling sad.

Animals have different skin like . . .
Stripes, spots, scales and fur
The dolphin moves quickly
The panda moves slowly.
The snake moves swiftly
And the cats moves creepily
I love all animals because they are different.

**Sophie Marsh  (8)**
**Willow Primary School**

# Sir Autumn

Prowling inside her leafy den, she grooms her mane of gold:
A lively creature, preparing to change the Earth.

Wearing her cloak of golden colours, she sweeps across the land,
Covering the ground in a warm blanket of fiery leaves.

Tumbling head over heels, crispy leaves scuttle across the path,
Whispering their secrets to Autumn's hissing breath.

Skeleton trees dance playfully in her calm, soothing breeze,
Relieved of their leaves, they wave their long, twisted arms.

Proud soldiers in spiky green armour - smooth, silky conkers
Emerge triumphantly from their dismal person cells.

Mischievous acorns rest deep beneath the dark, damp soil,
Playing hide-and-seek with their hungry predators.

Plump, juicy berries sit proudly in their prickly green seats,
Ripe, rosy apples search for somewhere to rest.

Outsider her leafy den, she admires her mane of gold:
A satisfied creature, Autumn has changed the Earth.

**Class 6W (Age 10 & 11)**
**Willow Primary School**


# Feelings

F eelings are normally good,
E veryone has them,
E ven parents!
L ife is a feeling sometimes it's tough, sometimes it's rough,
I sometimes feel like bursting with happiness
N othing explains things like feelings,
G oing away for a long time is a sad feeling,
S taying for a long time is a glad feeling.

**Max Green  (9)**
**Willow Primary School**

# Autumn

Autumn arrived today and took over summer,
She spread her cool weather over the Earth,
Wind and rain came at her command,
To cover the Earth.

Radiant leaves made a colourful blanket,
Over the long, soft grass,
Shades of gold, brown and orange,
Glow in the twilight.

Armour green clattered to the ground,
And revealed its innerself,
Old empty shells litter the ground,
Shiny conkers come out of hiding.

She paints the acorn a rich shade of gold,
They dance in her gentle breeze,
Scarecrows frighten hungry birds,
In to tall and proud trees.

**Simon Stockwell & Ralf Hudson  (10)**
**Willow Primary School**


# Autumn Days

Gently she blows her cool breath over the land
A powerful creature, ready to pounce.

Skeleton trees show their wrinkled arms in the swaying wind
Golden leaves shiver as they fall to the ground.

In their spiky green shells, smooth conkers sleep
Emerging from their dark home, they shine in the sun.

Acorns wear top hats and smart green suits,
Worried seeds try and find where they can stay the night.

Blowing her cold breath she stares at the dead land,
A happy creature who has just changed the Earth.

**Imogen Moore & Daniel Hassell  (10)**
**Willow Primary School**

# The Autumn Squirrel

Scurrying around his golden burrow,
Adding acorns to his pile,
Preparing for the season ahead.

The hazy sun shines down,
On Autumn's fiery home,
Gleaming through each crispy leaf.

Breathing on everything he sees,
Turning leaves from green to crimson,
He leaps eagerly from tree to tree.

Watching leaves drift elegantly to the ground,
Twisted trees smoothly sway in his warm breath,
Stripped bare but standing proud.

Carefully releasing themselves,
From their dark green cages,
Brown silky conkers lay under horse chestnut trees.

Relaxing in his golden burrow,
Eating acorns from his pile,
Autumn surrenders his power.

**Katie McGlone (10)**
**Willow Primary School**


# Feelings

F ull of mist, the playground is dull,
E ven the clouds are grey as cotton wool.
E verlasting the sky is grey,
L asting forever for the rest of the day,
I n the dull mist a figure emerges,
N ow it comes into my sight,
'G et some warm clothes on you look so white,'
S oon you can come to my house one night.

**Lewis Bennett (9)**
**Willow Primary School**

# Evil Autumn

Autumn came and whipped summer away
It massacred the leaves off the trees
and slaughtered the sun into temporary darkness,
roaring its ferocious wind at the defenceless trees.

Then it pelted down its icy ruins
and cloaked the blue sky in a grey blanket
Autumn soared forward leaving a trail of destruction,
the leaves charged forward like a soldier in battle.

Conkers break free from their spiky flesh,
revealing a glossy brown sphere,
vicious farmers rip up golden corn from their roots,
its Hallowe'en costumes haunt the Earth.

Crackling fires crackle all around,
the sky is filled with flashing fireworks,
as the last of autumn crawls by,
winter comes and whips autumn away.

**Ryan Lambert & Ryan Geldard (10)**
Willow Primary School

# Feelings

F riends can't tell you your feelings, only you can
E very day I remember I left my life behind,
E very so often I go to my room and think,
L ife is hard when there's something wrong,
I f there's something wrong with your feelings, tell someone,
N ever fear about your feelings or it gets worse,
G et some people and have a party at your house,
S ome people who are nice will be your friends.

**Courtney Chalk (9)**
Willow Primary School

# It Was The Worst Day Of Her Life

She was lonely and alone
No one was home
To comfort her at school

She sat in a corner
So sad
So scared
Like a hurricane hit her home

When it was drizzling with rain
She started in the toilets
And said to herself
'I'm never coming out!'

But then she heard somebody
Coming towards her
It was a girl . . . she asked her
If she wanted to play

So really was it the worst day of her life?

**Jordenne Murray  (10)**
**Willow Primary School**


# Raindrops

Raindrops down the window
The weather's wet and dull
I feel like I'm falling
I'm starting a new school

Raindrops from my eyes
I wish someone would come to me
To take me from dark light
And put me in the sun

Raindrops down the window
The weather's wet and dull
Now I'm not falling
I'm having fun at my new school.

**Grace Wood  (9)**
**Willow Primary School**

# Rainbow Feelings

Red is angry,
She needs to calm down,
Count to ten,
Put a smile on that frown.

Orange is happy,
He brightens up the days,
Everyone is happy,
When he shines his rays.

Yellow is thoughtful,
To everyone in town,
Maybe red should meet her,
To turn her frown around.

Green is calm,
He cools you down,
When you've been running,
All over town.

Blue is sad,
She cries all day,
Never mind orange,
The tears won't go away.

Indigo is kind,
She gives flowers to everyone,
Everyone is sad,
When she is gone.

Violet is jealous,
He wishes he was green,
Everyone around him says,
'He's always been so keen.'

**Robyn Gunn (9)**
**Willow Primary School**

# Autumn's Revenge

Twitching his golden nose, he senses it's time to reappear,
Shaking his fiery tail he launches himself into the air.

Thrusting sweltering summer out of the way,
He begins his revenge on the Earth.

Harvesting crinkled leaves from jealous trees,
He throws crimson colours across the land.

Charging at weak, resisting fences,
Demolishing them with his violent breath.

Forcing silky brown conkers to leap from trees,
Leaving their spiky green armour behind.

Grasping his icy reins, he freezes the world,
Winter lashes his icicle whip round the yelping fox.

**Georgia Lakin & Duncan Haddrell  (10)**
**Willow Primary School**


# Autumn Days

Stroking the Earth with her golden hand,
She blows fiery colours across the land.

Bare trees dancing with gentle breeze,
Sway side to side with greatest ease.

Tumbling leaves race down slippery slopes,
Shiny, smooth conkers in spiky coats.

Touching trees with beautiful fingers,
Layers of leaves gather and linger.

Carelessly throwing water on fading leaves,
Intense pitter-patter pounding at eaves.

Waving goodbye with her icy hand,
She slowly disappears from the darkening land.

**Chloe Cope & Sophia Arjomand  (11)**
**Willow Primary School**

# Autumn

A chameleon inside her secret den,
She plans to control the Earth,
Reaching for her magical cloak, she prepares for her special journey.

Breathing blustery winds, she tickles the vibrant leaves,
Scattering them across the colourful floor,
Turning them into a golden whirlpool.

Strong, prickly armour shields shiny polished conkers,
Protecting them from hungry predators,
Dropping to the ground, they break free and emerge.

With no time to play, animals scurry,
Panicking like frightened ants,
Hiding nuts and berries for the long winter ahead.

A chameleon inside her secret den,
She has conquered the Earth,
Removing her magical cloak, her special journey has ended.

**Jenny Collins  (11) & James Peach  (10)**
**Willow Primary School**


# Autumn Fox

Creeping around her fiery hideout like a sly fox,
She plans to change the Earth.

Jealous trees cry, spitting dancing leaves, showing their
                                        twisted arms,
Autumn sheds her red fur.

Bursting from spiky armour, conkers screech as they punch
                                        the damp ground,
She grasps them in her chilly breath.

Playing hide-and-seek with their giddy predators,
Nervous acorns scurry to the underground.

Sleeping outside her golden hideout like a proud hero,
Autumn has changed the Earth.

**Danny Young  (10) & Becky Smith**
**Willow Primary School**

# Fiery Autumn

Summer dies, the sun smiles faintly,
Colourful autumn takes over.

Crispy leaves roll down steep hills,
Racing for survival.

Dancing trees wave their arms frantically,
Losing crunchy golden leaves.

Spiky green armour protects smooth conkers,
Excitedly they burst open.

Juicy fruits hang on rough branches,
Inviting someone to pick them.

Autumn fades away, crunchy leaves disappear,
Cold-blooded winter takes over.

**Joshua Bennett  (10) & Emma Phagra**
**Willow Primary School**


# Autumn

Washing her face with her golden soap,
She sighs with colourful breath.

A fierce creature pouncing on the Earth,
She squeezes with her powerful hands.

Bullying the weakening trees,
She steals their crispy leaves.

Covering the lush grass,
She kills the beautiful flowers.

Falling in their green armour,
The conkers break from their long sleep.

**Olivia Binns & Afnan Rabbani  (10)**
**Willow Primary School**

# The Russet Sergeant

A russet sergeant ordering her troops,
She takes control of the land.

Summer releases her scorching grasp,
A fiery creature takes up the reins.

With claws of gold she strips the trees,
Leaving them vulnerable and alone.

A carpet of crunchy, dry leaves,
Covers the path with rusty colours.

Proud soldiers break out at last,
Revealing their brown silky skin.

Spiky hedgehogs quickly prepare,
For their long rest in their leafy den.

Cool breezes dance with the twisted arms of the dying trees,
Begging for mercy once again.

Autumn is gripped by talons of ice:
Wild winter now preys on the Earth.

**Lewis Mycock & Ellie Neil  (11)**
**Willow Primary School**

# Young Writers Information

We hope you have enjoyed reading this book - and that you will continue to enjoy it in the coming years.

If you like reading and writing poetry drop us a line, or give us a call, and we'll send you a free information pack.

Alternatively if you would like to order further copies of this book or any of our other titles, then please give us a call or log onto our website at
www.youngwriters.co.uk

**Young Writers Information
Remus House
Coltsfoot Drive
Peterborough
PE2 9JX**

**(01733) 890066**